*Also by Stedman Graham*

You Can Make It Happen
You Can Make It Happen
    Every Day
Teens Can Make It Happen

# BUILD YOUR OWN LIFE BRAND!

*A Powerful Strategy to*
*Maximize Your Potential*
*and Enhance Your Value*
*for Ultimate Achievement*

STEDMAN GRAHAM

A FIRESIDE BOOK

Published by Simon & Schuster

New York London Toronto Sydney Singapore

Fireside
Rockefeller Center
1230 Avenue of the Americas
New York, NY 10020

First Fireside Edition 2002

FIRESIDE and colophon are registered trademarks of Simon & Schuster, Inc.

For information about special discounts for bulk purchases,
please contact Simon & Schuster Special Sales at 1-800-456-6798
or business@simonandschuster.com

Designed by Elina D. Nudelman

Manufactured in the United States of America

10 9 8 7 6 5 4 3 2 1

The Library of Congress has cataloged the Free Press edition as follows:
Graham, Stedman.
Build your own life brand! : a powerful strategy to maximize your potential
and enhance your value for ultimate achievement / Stedman Graham.
p.   cm.
1. Success—Psychological aspects.  I. Title.
BF637.S8 G683    2001
158—dc21          00-050295

ISBN 0-684-85697-2
     0-684-85698-0 (Pbk)

*To Oprah, whose life brand is exemplary.*
*The magnitude of your success*
*is surpassed only by that of your heart.*

# Acknowledgments

Those who are familiar with my first book, *You Can Make It Happen,* will know that *Build Your Own Life Brand!* complements and expands upon the ideas set forth in that book. In *You Can Make It Happen,* readers learn a systematic approach to achieving success, evaluating your strengths, and using that knowledge to formulate a life strategy. *Build Your Own Life Brand!* provides the tools to look at oneself as a brand, using the concepts that marketers and advertisers use to express your character and values to friends, colleagues, and acquaintances in an honest and positive light.

I want to thank writer Wes Smith for his skill in expressing the ideas in this book. I'm also grateful to the many family members, friends, and business associates who have contributed—and continue to contribute—to my success. Particularly generous in advising me and helping to expand my understanding of corporate America have been my personal dream team: my father, the late Stedman Graham, Sr., as well as my uncles Lewis and Tom Graham, who provided my first exposure to business—part of the Graham family tradition; my friend and mentor Bob Brown; Dominick Anfuso; Tolbert Chisum; Grant Gregory; Jim Hayes; Steve Lesnik; Jan Miller; Chuck Peebler; Armstrong Williams; and Val Zammit. These people set the standards that I seek to meet as I build my own business.

# Contents

# Build a Brand Name for Yourself

CHAPTER ONE

WHEN I WAS playing high school basketball many years ago, there was one name that stood out in every game: Chuck Taylor. Chuck wasn't a big scorer or a great rebounder. In fact, he was constantly underfoot on the court. More accurately, he was *on our feet*. Before there were Nikes or Reeboks, Converse Chuck Taylor All Stars was *the* brand. It was the most popular basketball shoe of my high school generation.

Back then, when you made the varsity team, you just had to get a pair of Chuck Taylor high-tops. All the players that I admired in high school, college, and the pros were wearing them, so I associated Chuck Taylor with success on the basketball court. I grew up like everyone else, with hundreds of other brand-name products around me—top brands such as Wheaties, Pepsi, and Ford Thunderbird—but my desire to have a pair of Chuck Taylors marked the real beginning of my *brand awareness* as a consumer.

A brand product is one with a unique identity intended to set it apart from similar products. The cereal brand Wheaties is "the breakfast of champions." The Pepsi soft drink brand is "the joy of cola." Compaq brand computers offer "better answers," according to an ad in a magazine on my desk. We are so bombarded by product brands that we are hardly conscious of them much of the time, but most of us have at least some level of brand awareness. We can sing the jingles of our favorite brands. *It's the real thing!* We can repeat their ad slogans. *Just do it!* Most important for the companies that make brand-name products, we look for them when we shop.

Increasing a product's brand awareness is one of the jobs performed by my management and marketing consulting company, S. Graham & Associates. Marketing and working with brands are the primary roles of my firm, which provides strategic planning, marketing, consulting, and program execution to companies seeking to target general and multicultural markets. Our clients come to us for help in creating, expanding, and revitalizing their brand names. Our speciality is to build upon what they have already accomplished with their brands by helping them sell their products to multicultural consumers whom they may not be reaching effectively. We also help new companies develop and establish their brands by determining what their primary target markets are and how they can best explain the value of their product to consumers.

## A BRAND-NEW WAY OF LOOKING AT YOUR LIFE

o "Everything is a brand. Most people don't recognize that. Where you live, the house you live in, the street you live on . . . they are all brands. And people are brands," Frank Delano, president of the New York–based Delano & Young, a brand-image firm, told the *Chicago Tribune* recently.

o "We're all brands, in the sense that we have a certain identity, have to maintain a certain quality and have to bring something to [radio station] affiliates they can't bring to themselves," said broadcaster Charles Osgood at a 1999 advertising industry conference entitled "Brand Building for the 21st Century."

The business world has long recognized the value of creating a recognizable and clearly defined brand. In recent years, the principles of branding increasingly have been applied to individuals too. Just as Coca-Cola, Apple, and Tommy Hilfiger have brands with assets that they develop and pitch to consumers, you too have assets that you must build upon, market, and expand. It may sound strange to you at first, but think about these situations:

o When you apply for a job, aren't you trying to "sell" the interviewer on you and your particular brand assets, which include your talents, knowledge, training, and personal characteristics such as your energy, your determination, or your leadership attributes?

o When you meet someone whom you find interesting or attractive, don't you try to make a favorable impression so that you will stand out in that person's mind?

o When you move into a new neighborhood, join an organization, or participate in a fund-raising drive, don't you try to communicate to the people involved that you have something of value to offer?

While the concept of branding yourself may seem strange at first, I've noticed that many successful people instinctively think of themselves as "brands" or "products" in the marketplace. When I told Oprah that I had decided to write a book on personal branding, she said: "People are always talking about how I built my *brand* but I wasn't thinking about that at all. I was winging it, just trying to do my best and to get where I wanted to be." Today, Oprah is very aware of her brand as a businesswoman and entertainer, as are most other successful men and women. They may have built their brands instinctively, but they realize the importance of managing them thoughtfully.

Each of us has a unique blend of talents, knowledge, and other personal assets. We want to make the most of those gifts by developing them and sharing them with the world. I believe that's what makes us truly happy. It isn't about having the nicest clothes, the fanciest cars, or the biggest house. Happiness comes when you are fully engaged in life, so that when you come to the end of your time on this earth, you've used up every ounce of energy, every bit of brainpower, and every gift you've been given. The happiest, most fulfilled people I know aren't necessarily those with the most material things. They are the people who know that their lives have value in the world around them.

When you build a *Life Brand,* and then manage it, expand upon it, and protect it, you create a method for sharing your gifts and putting them to their highest use—for your benefit and for the benefit of everyone within your reach. Did you notice I called your brand a "Life Brand"? That's because my goal is to help you attain your highest potential and value, not only in your work or career but also in your relationships, and in every other aspect of your life.

You have talents, knowledge, and other gifts to share—not just at work, but with your loved ones and with everyone who shares some portion of your life. In the chapters that follow, we will assess your Life Brand "assets," and then look at ways to increase and enhance your value in everything you become involved in. The ultimate goal is to create a fulfilling life by enriching the lives of everyone you touch. It's built upon the philosophy that when you focus on offering your talents and energy to serve others, the rewards will flow your way too.

## A BRAND TO BUILD YOUR LIFE AROUND

*Branding* has long been a buzzword in the business world, but I'm going to take you beyond creating a mere career brand. My vision of personal branding differs substantially from visions that basically offer methods for promoting yourself in your job or career. It's wonderful to be successful in your work, but I've seen too many people who focus only on getting to the top, neglecting their relationships and their personal development along the way. Often, they achieve their goals and then realize that they feel emotionally and spiritually empty because their focus has been too narrow. As Lily Tomlin said, "The trouble with the rat race is that even if you win, you're still a rat."

There is no real or lasting fulfillment in a life focused merely on obtaining material success, power, or recognition. There is nothing inherently wrong with those things, if they happen to come to you as the result of how you live your life. I believe they should not be your primary goal. "The less I've cared about money and commissions, the more money I've made. Make the right decisions for the right reasons and the right things will happen. Remember: He who dies with the most toys . . . dies," says Bill Haber, who cofounded the Creative Artists Agency and is now active in the Save the Children charity.

Like Bill Haber, I've found that the most fulfilled people are those who build value into their Life Brands and then spread it around. I'm going to show you in the pages that follow how to create a high-quality Life Brand that will enable you to stand out not only in your work but also in your relationships and the greater "communities" that you belong to. I consider your communities to include everything from the place you live and the world you live in to your professional ties, your spiritual life, and your network of friends, business associates, teammates, and anyone else within your circle of influence. That includes service, religious, professional, and social organizations; charities, fraternities, and sororities; and your own network of contacts and acquaintances.

## SAY "YOU FIRST" AND YOU WILL BENEFIT TOO

I have another concern about many of the personal branding programs I've seen. They often encourage a "me first" attitude. It's not you and your brand against the world. That approach will get you nowhere fast. Why would an employer or client, a friend, or a teammate buy into someone with that approach? I prefer to think of personal branding as a method for identifying your value as a human being, for making that value widely known, and for nurturing and enhancing that value throughout your lifetime.

Here's a quick exercise to help you see the difference between branding yourself purely for selfish reasons and building a Life Brand for the purpose of sharing your talents, skills, and knowledge with the world:

*Visualize yourself seated in the middle of a huge crowd in an auditorium. Many of the most powerful people in politics, entertainment, and business are present. There are television cameras positioned to broadcast the evening's events to viewing audiences around the world. With all of the influential people and media on hand, it's a great opportunity to "sell" your Life Brand. But how?*

*Here are two options:*

1. You stand on the seat of your chair and jump up and down while shouting for attention and then you tell everyone what you've done and what you have to offer.

   Or . . .

2. The master of ceremonies asks everyone else in the audience to rise and honor you with their applause and cheers for your many accomplishments and contributions.

Which scenario appeals to you? Which would have the most far-reaching and long-lasting implications? Which would be more rewarding over the long term? *That* is the difference between mere self-promotion and Life Brand building. Unlike some personal branding methods, mine is designed to help you put your talents, skills, knowledge, and personal strengths to their greatest use in the service of your employers or clients, your loved ones, and your community. That does not mean that I'm advising you to give your gifts away. On the contrary, my belief is that when we focus on adding value to others, we realize more rewards than we would ever receive by seeking only personal success, wealth, or recognition. Of course, the first thing you must do is build up your own "assets." That's what creating a Life Brand is all about.

This book offers guidance to help you identify the best that is within you by building a Life Brand with valuable assets. You will learn how to build your brand based on who you *really* are, not who you think people might want you to be. Much of the current literature on personal branding talks about "selling" yourself to potential employers, clients, or customers. Be assured, I am not going to show you how to sell yourself like a box of Cheer or a six-pack of Yoo-Hoo soft drink. I will offer you a variety of proven methods to market your Life Brand in order to help you stretch for even greater opportunities and challenges.

We all want to stand out from the crowd. We all want to lead meaningful and fulfilling lives. We all want to be successful in our own way. I will help you do those things by teaching you to think of yourself as a Life Brand. This is more than a catchphrase or a motivational tool. It's a method for managing your life. My process is a *holistic* approach encompassing all aspects of your life. It will keep you focused on the things that are truly unique about you and important to you. It will help you maintain a balance among work, family, and service to your community. It also will be of great use when you are faced with making important decisions, by helping you distinguish between those opportunities that are in alignment with your long-term goals for all aspects of your Life Brand and those that are not.

Before we get into the process of building your Life Brand, let's take a deeper look at the concept of product branding. Not everything done in the branding of consumer products applies to people, of course, but many of the principles are the same, and it will be helpful for you to understand the basics.

## THE POWER OF A BRAND

When you are looking for clothes do you seek out brand names like FUBU, Gap, or Donna Karan? At the grocery store, do you purchase generic ketchup or Heinz? Odds are that you have picked up an affinity for one brand or another in almost every type of goods you purchase. You're still not sure that you have any brand preferences? Do you like bananas? One banana tastes pretty much like any other banana, doesn't it? I have one word for you—Chiquita—a brand-name banana. They grow on the same trees as all other bananas, but because they've got a well-known, heavily marketed brand name, you and I tend to choose them over bananas sold by other producers.

What makes for a powerful product brand? In 1997, Interbrand, a branding consulting firm with clients around the world, published an analysis of top brands. The company evaluated 350 brands using four criteria. As you read these, think about how each of them might apply to your Life Brand in your three primary markets: your work, your relationships, and the greater communities that you participate in.

The four criteria for a strong brand as identified by Interbrand were:

1. *Brand weight:* the brand's *influence* in its category or market
2. *Brand length:* its *reach* outside its original category

3. *Brand breadth:* its *appeal range* in terms of age groups, consumer types, and international impact
4. *Brand depth:* its ability to *inspire loyalty* among consumers

Based on those four criteria, Interbrand selected its top ten consumer product brands. Before you read the list, make up your own based on the brand names that are most familiar to you. The names on your list probably will match those on Interbrand's fairly closely if you have a typical level of brand awareness. Here are their choices for the top ten consumer product brands:

1. *McDonald's,* which was cited for its "consistent brand values, industry dominance, and a living personality"
2. *Coca-Cola,* a brand with "worldwide appeal"
3. *Disney,* known for its "integrated system in which each Disney property enhances and reinforces the whole"
4. *Kodak,* a major brand since 1888
5. *Sony,* a brand with a "clear focus on electronics, technical research and innovation, and a policy of global localization"
6. *Gillette,* another long-term brand that has updated its image in recent years
7. *Mercedes-Benz,* "the ultimate status brand embodying safety, heritage, and longevity"
8. *Levi's,* a dominant brand that has struggled recently but still is strongly linked with American values
9. *Microsoft,* a relatively new brand that has grown from a software leader to a much broader technology brand
10. *Marlboro,* "the world's leading international cigarette brand, instantly recognizable by its red and white packaging and cowboy image"

## STRONG BRANDS DELIVER ON THEIR PROMISE

The companies behind all of those brand-name products and the millions of others being pitched to you each day believe that a strong brand creates a bond with consumers by giving them something of *value* and by consistently delivering on their *promise* of doing it. When you go into a McDonald's restaurant—whether it's in Boise, Idaho; Bangor, Maine; or Brownsville, Texas—you know what to expect. That Quarter Pounder with Cheese that you value so much will be there, and its taste will be consistent with those that you've had at other McDonald's. Companies with powerful brands have learned that you and I will keep coming back to their products, and sometimes pay a premium price for them, if they consistently deliver on that promise of giving us something we want or need.

Think for a minute about the people you value most in your work, your relationships, and within organizations or groups you belong to. They are people who deliver something you value, aren't they? They have skills, knowledge, or personal characteristics that add to the quality of your life. Their "brands" or reputations carry a promise. Do you have an employee or a coworker who comes through every time? A trusted adviser whose wisdom you rely upon? A favorite aunt or uncle whom you can always count upon to make you feel loved and appreciated? A friend who makes you laugh even in down times? Each of those individuals offers something specific that you value. The people who mean the most to you, then, are those who offer you the most value throughout your life. The individuals who stand out in the world around us are those who offer the greatest value to the most people—just as those products with the strongest brands are the ones that offer us the greatest value.

## BRAND BEGINNINGS

Modern marketing experts attribute the development of *brand images* for products to the advertising world. David Ogilvy, one of the masterminds of advertising in the 1960s, and the author of *Confessions of an Advertising Man,* popularized the idea of creating a lasting brand image for products in order to create customer loyalty for the long term. Ogilvy believed in selling not just the product but also the physical or psychological benefits that are "promised" in the product's advertising and marketing. His approach led to the creation of the Marlboro Man and the Pepsi Generation brand images, among many others.

Ogilvy and his disciples in the advertising and marketing game believed that what was said or promised about the product through the brand image was every bit as important, if not more important, than the actual product itself. You and I don't always buy into this consciously, but subconsciously we may select a certain brand of car, say a Jeep Grand Cherokee, over another brand, say a Chevrolet Suburban, because the Jeep has a brand image that we find more appealing—even though both models would satisfy our basic needs for getting to work, the grocery store, and the soccer game.

## BRANDS FOR A LIFESTYLE

Today, it is all but impossible not to have the big brand names dancing in your brain because of all the brand advertising in newspapers and magazines, and on billboards, radio, television, and the Internet. Some of it is meaningful, but some of it is downright silly. If you read some computer ads, it sounds as though they are selling race cars, not desktops. But there is a method to this madness. It's all about associating a desirable image with a product in order to attract consumers to the product.

Some brand marketers talk about creating a *lifestyle brand*. Marketing scientists who study consumer buying habits say that brands can become so powerful that people incorporate them into their everyday lives. That's why you see the Eddie Bauer brand not only on rugged clothing but also on casual home furnishings, bedding, baby furniture, rugs, candles, lanterns, lamps, and garden accessories, not to mention a special edition of the Ford Explorer.

Once a brand becomes as well established as Eddie Bauer, the people who own it do their best to extend its reach so that it becomes a lifestyle choice. That means creating new products that bear the brand name and joining forces with other major brands, such as Ford, to reach entirely new markets.

From my experiences in the marketing business, I can tell you that successful companies like Eddie Bauer and others such as Johnson & Johnson, which makes and sells big brand-name products such as Tylenol, Motrin, and Band-Aid, spend millions and millions of dollars creating, advertising, and building their brand names so that you and I will ask for their products.

These giant companies understand the long-term benefits of building a brand that stands out from the crowd. *So should you!*

*But I'm not selling anything,* you say. That is not true.

## BRANDING YOURSELF

If you have any goals or dreams for your life, then, whether you realize it or not, you are already pitching your own "brand" every day in many different ways—whether you are a high school student hoping to make the grade for college, an athlete vying for a position on a team, or a businessperson working to get ahead of the competition. You may never have thought of applying the branding process to your life, but others have been doing it for years. Candidates for public office have been packaged like brands since the days of "Honest Abe" and "Give 'Em Hell, Harry" Truman. Franklin Delano Roosevelt was packaged as a dynamic, athletic presidential candidate even though he was generally confined to a wheelchair. John F. Kennedy's brand managers frequently arranged for the press to photograph him playing touch football or roughhousing with his children, yet we later learned he had such a bad back that he often had to sit in a rocking chair.

What about brand-name celebrities? As I'll show you in a later chapter, they have been packaged and branded since the earliest days of Hollywood, when studio actors and actresses were given whole new identities in order to sell them to the press and the public. Today, the concept of personal branding—creating a distinctive identity that makes a person stand out from the crowd—has become so widely used that headhunters, college advisers, and career counselors encourage job hunters to "package themselves" as a brand in the workforce marketplace.

Why is branding a good idea for you? Because the world of work has changed, and because, as I've discovered, it's a wonderful way to take responsibility for your own happiness and success in all aspects of your life.

In bygone agricultural and industrial societies, people's lives were generally charted out from birth. The majority of men and women never left the villages or cities where they were born. Most stayed within the jobs or professions and class levels of their parents. The world was a smaller place. People typically knew each other from birth. They knew each other's families from generation to generation.

That is no longer the case in our *knowledge* society. Today we are fairly bombarded with choices and opportunities. It's increasingly rare to know where you will be living or working ten or even five years into the future. Class mobility has also hit hyperspeed. A fast move up can come with a surge in the NASDAQ, a bonus check, or a job offer that includes stock options. We are always on the move, and as a result, it is more difficult to let others know the value we represent as individuals. That is why it is now so important to take responsibility for managing every aspect of your life. It's not so much about having control. Nobody can control what happens *to* them, but we can control how we respond. Building a Life Brand helps you to understand your own strengths and your own weaknesses. It encourages you to keep building upon your strengths throughout your lifetime so that you are prepared to take advantage of the opportunities that most appeal to you. A well-defined personal brand will also help you more easily determine which opportunities don't fit into your life plan and which ones are worth pursuing because they fit into your long-term goals.

## THE MARK OF AN ACHIEVER

When you create, manage, and keep expanding your Life Brand, it gives you an advantage over those who simply drift along, or get swept away by the tide. "History's great achievers—a Napoleon, a da Vinci, a Mozart—have always managed themselves. That, in large measure, is what makes them great achievers," notes management expert Peter F. Drucker in a *Harvard Business Review* article entitled "Managing Oneself."

"Now, most of us, even those of us with modest endowments, will have to learn to manage ourselves. We will have to learn to develop ourselves. We will have to place ourselves where we can make the greatest contribution," he added. "Managing oneself demands that each knowledge worker think and behave like a chief executive."

Creating a Life Brand provides you with a system for doing just that. It positions you as the head of your own company whose primary product is *your life.* The goal of your Life Brand Inc. is to create a fulfilling and productive existence, one you hope will be valued long after you've gone.

The father of product branding, David Ogilvy, died in July 1999 at the age of eighty-eight. One month later, the company he founded in 1948—the giant advertising firm of Ogilvy & Mather Worldwide—announced that it was remaking its corporate identity by adopting the handwritten signature of Ogilvy as its official logo. "We've embraced the truth about the brand known as Ogilvy; humor, uniqueness, boldness, individuality," said one of the firm's executives in a news story. David Ogilvy's Life Brand was so strong that even after his death this global corporation chose to link itself to him and the integrity and high standards his name still represents.

My goal in writing this book is to help you build *that* kind of life: one that people will remember, respect, and honor long after you've moved on.

Let's get started.

# Life Brand Management 101

## CHAPTER TWO

**I WAS DISCUSSING** the concept of Life Branding with a coworker recently, and he offered someone up as a great example. His friend unconsciously followed the Life Branding process and achieved remarkable results. He transformed his passion into a great career, and perhaps best of all, for the first time in his life, this person began to take real pleasure in his work and his life. This is a true story. The individual, whose first name is Tom, asked that I not use his full name because he doesn't feel he has accomplished "anything special." I'll let you judge that. I happen to believe one of the greatest things you and I can accomplish is to identify what it is that we are most passionate about doing, and then to build our lives around it and share it with the world. When you create a Life Brand, identify your brand assets, and devote yourself to developing them to their greatest potential, you put yourself in a position to accomplish what Tom has done.

Tom was a good student in high school, a real whiz at math, but he didn't have any sense of direction for his life, no goals, no passion, nor any dreams to guide him. He went to a small community college and earned only a two-year degree in electronics. While still in his twenties, he was working as a car stereo installer in a small Midwestern college town. By his own admission, he was simply drifting along in life. He was un-motivated and unfulfilled. When the revolution in home com-puters hit, Tom discovered something that excited and intrigued him. "It was more accidental than it was on pur-pose," he said. "I was just kind of wandering aimlessly through life not really knowing what I wanted to do, or caring that much, and I just sort of fell into doing this."

Unlike most of us who are happy to use the computer as a word processor, for playing computer games, or as a way to surf the Internet, Tom became intrigued by the inner work-ings of computers, particularly the writing of computer soft-ware. He had taken a few computer science classes in school, but most of the things he learned were ancient history by the time his interest grew. He began reading books on computer processing to increase his knowledge and bring himself up to date. He taught himself how to write programs, and mastered the complexities of a number of computer languages without any help.

Tom's search for more knowledge to feed his growing passion led him to take a series of jobs with several small soft-ware companies in his community. When he talked about his ideas with coworkers, they suggested he share his unique ap-proaches with a wider audience, so he began writing articles for computer magazines. Tom didn't do any of this for money, or ambition, or glory. He did it because he had a passion for it. Even though he had married and was thinking about starting a family, Tom still didn't have a plan for his life or his career as he reached his late thirties. Slowly, unconsciously, though, he began building a brand in what was rapidly turning into the hottest industry on the planet. "I did make a decision five or six years ago that I would concentrate on writing software for Windows because I thought it was going to be the dominant operating system," he said. "So, whenever projects would pop up wherever I was working, I would try to work on those related to Windows. I was just following my muse as far as what I was doing and writing magazine articles and such. I just had some ideas and people told me they were cool so I wrote about them."

Tom was working in a low-key job for a small software company three years ago when the owners announced that they were moving their entire operation to the West Coast. He was offered a position at the new location, but Tom took the opportunity to stop and assess his life. When he did, he realized it might be time to test his value in the larger market. Again, he wasn't thinking consciously about "branding" himself, but that is exactly what he had done while using his natural talents and pursuing his interests in computer science.

Tom had built considerable value into his brand by teaching himself how to perform complex software-writing tasks. His growing expertise also created a promise that he could consistently come up with unique approaches. He had unconsciously marketed his brand by writing about his work for national magazines. He did all this because he had discovered a passion for computer technologies. When it came time to look for another job, he looked to the market leader in his field because he wanted to measure himself against the best. "I'd always thought Microsoft software was cool and I thought they were doing the right things. I like to work in shorts and T-shirts and do my work without a lot of hand-holding and I'd read that they had that kind of environment for their software designers, so I e-mailed my résumé to them."

Within a few weeks, Microsoft flew the former car radio installer to Seattle for four long and grueling days of interviews and intense testing. He began to feel early on in the interviewing process that he had a good shot at getting a job with the industry giant because of the assets he had unconsciously built into his brand. "I had mentioned in the résumé that I'd written software for VxD Windows device drivers and I guess that got their attention because during my interview one of their people said that they thought no one outside of Microsoft knew how to write for that particular driver. I think they were impressed that I had figured it out."

His instincts were correct. After Tom returned home, a Microsoft recruiter called and said that two competing project groups within the company wanted him to work for them. After some negotiating, Tom accepted an offer that would dramatically change both the quality and the pace of his life.

## BUILDING A LIFE BRAND PREPARES YOU
## FOR OPPORTUNITIES

Tom is a modest person. He claims things simply "fell into place" for him. That is really not the case. "Successful careers are not planned. They develop when people are prepared for opportunities because they know their strengths, their methods of work and their values. Knowing where one belongs can transform an ordinary person . . . into an outstanding performer," management expert Peter Drucker has noted.

Mr. Drucker could have been writing about Tom, who unconsciously followed the process of building a Life Brand and is now reaping the rewards. Tom pursued his passion by building on his natural strengths. He worked hard but it didn't really seem like "work" because it deeply interested and excited him. He built value into his brand by educating himself and mastering technical tasks that brought him the respect of the tech wizards at Microsoft. After he'd built up his "brand assets," Tom then identified the sort of work environment he wanted and he pursued the opportunities open to him at the No. 1 company in his profession.

Not surprisingly, Tom established his brand very quickly at Microsoft. In his first three years, he earned a patent for a software design he created. Other high-tech companies began inviting him to speak to their employees around the country and abroad. Although he has only a two-year degree from a community college, Tom now finds himself delivering lectures to fellow information-technology professionals with doctoral degrees in computer science.

*That's* the power of identifying a passion and building on your strengths to create a valuable Life Brand!

Understand that I don't believe you have to land a high-paying job with Microsoft to consider yourself successful or to be happy or fulfilled. Building a Life Brand is not about achieving status, wealth, or fame. It's about taking responsibility for your own happiness and fulfillment. It's about creating a life of value by putting your gifts to their highest use.

Tom says that money and material success have never been a priority in his life. He merely was looking for a way to apply his intelligence, creativity, and energy. For him, the far more important thing is that he now has built a career that fulfills him. He is no longer drifting. He is fully engaged in the flow of life. "Although the financial rewards and professional success are interesting, to tell you the truth, the fun and happiness in my life are really all I care about," he said. "It's taken a long time for me to be really happy in what I do for a living and it was worth the wait. I guess a lot of this goes back to following your muse and doing what you are passionate about."

Tom did that. Unconsciously, he built value for himself and then marketed a brand that has taken him to the top of his field, where he will be able to keep following his muse. By educating himself, Tom also built up his self-confidence, which also benefited him in his work and relationships. Isn't that what happiness is about—chasing your dreams, building a life of value, and following opportunities that bring fulfillment in every aspect of your existence?

## TRANSCENDING YOUR SELF BY BUILDING A BRAND

I serve on nonprofit and charity boards, and I'm frequently surprised at the number of truly wealthy men and women who give their time and energy to help others. Most could spend the rest of their lives playing golf, lounging by the pool, or traveling the world. Why do you suppose they choose to offer themselves to the service of others instead? I've asked some of them, and their answers are generally very similar. They do it because they don't believe they are really successful until they help others find opportunities too. Even in Tom's case, when he talks about his work, it's not about how he has benefited personally; he is far more excited about the *contribution* he is making to the world of computing science, which fascinates him.

Much of the material on personal branding encourages the development of an individual's unique potential in the workplace. That's a worthy goal, but it is ultimately not a ful-filling one because it deals with only one small aspect of your life. Have you ever heard it said that someone who is totally wrapped up in himself makes for a very small package? When you create a Life Brand, you are putting together a much larger package. It's not just about you. It's about everything and everyone you come into contact with. The goal of your Life Brand is to create what psychologists call "the transcen-dent self."

"It involves becoming aware of, and in control of, one's unique potentials, and being able to create harmony between goals and desires, sensations and experiences, both for one-self and for others. People who achieve this are not only going to have a more fulfilling life, but they are almost certainly more likely to contribute to a better future. Personal happi-ness and a positive contribution to evolution go hand in hand," notes the University of Chicago psychologist Mihaly Csikszentmihaly in *The Evolving Self.*

I've been blessed in my life to know people of all types, all economic classes, all levels of education, all colors and faiths. There are incredible success stories across every one of those categories and lifestyles. One thing many of these people have in common is that they believe in using their talents, knowl-edge, skills, and personal attributes to bring value to the world around them.

You can have all the valuables. I'll take a life of value in-stead, one that transcends self-interest and offers me the op-portunity to make a difference in the lives of others. There are a great many people who are "just drifting" as Tom said. There are probably more who get caught up in the hunt for personal success and self-recognition but feel empty inside. Then there are those with powerful Life Brands who happily use their unique gifts to create a better future not only for themselves but for others too.

## A LIFE BRAND THAT HEALS
## BROKEN CHILDHOODS

Brenda Eheart was a professor and expert in child welfare at the University of Illinois in Urbana when she and another professor undertook a seven-year study of "unadoptable" foster children. These are kids who never know a permanent home. Often they have complex physical or mental problems. Sometimes they are simply part of a group of foster siblings who cannot be split up. In their study, the professors found that these "unadoptable" children usually are bounced from one foster home to the next. Once they reach adulthood, they face even greater difficulty. A high percentage end up in trouble with the law, institutionalized, or, tragically, as suicides.

Brenda Eheart and her partner completed their study, but instead of simply publishing their findings in a scholarly journal and then moving on to other academic work, Eheart became determined to take action. She had once worked as a counselor to families in Chicago's public housing projects, where she witnessed what happens when one generation after another fails to find a way out of poverty and despair. She knew that unless the "unadoptable" children were removed from that cycle and given an opportunity to join mainstream society, there was little hope for them or their children and grandchildren.

Brenda Eheart was already a well-established academic. She had her own family, including one adopted child, to look after in addition to her teaching and research. Yet, she was compelled to do more than study this problem and report on it. She wanted to add value to the lives of these children. She wanted to help them reach their potential and make their own contributions to the world.

For nearly two years, Brenda and a group of equally concerned people developed a plan for giving the unadoptable foster children a chance at a "normal" life. Often, Brenda and her friends thought that there was little chance for their dream to become a reality. They had no money. No political clout. No powerful connections.

Brenda did have a powerful Life Brand, one whose assets included intelligence, compassion, integrity, and a fierce determination. When people saw her unselfish commitment to bringing value to the lives of neglected and unwanted children, they bought into Brenda's brand. Somehow, she convinced reluctant officials of the military bureaucracy at the Pentagon and the U.S. Air Force to share her vision for creating an entire community devoted to helping the neediest children in foster care. They agreed to sell Brenda and her nonprofit foundation sixty-five duplex apartments on twenty-two acres of the closed Chanute Field Air Force Training Base in Rantoul, Illinois.

Brenda raised $215,000 for the purchase as part of a $1 million grant she secured through the Illinois Department of Children and Family Services. She got that money with the help of a most unlikely coalition of Democrats, Republicans, social workers, lawyers, businesspeople, child care advocates, and academics. All of them came together because of the power of Brenda's purpose and passion.

Today, on the former military air base, she has created Hope Meadows, a community devoted to restoring the childhoods and creating futures for young people who might otherwise never find permanent or loving homes. More than forty of those children now live at Hope Meadows, which opened in 1994. Most of them will be permanently adopted by families brought to Hope Meadows by Brenda's vision. The families are supported by a team of psychologists, child therapists, and other professionals who either live at or regularly visit Hope Meadows. They are also backed up by nearly sixty "foster grandparents," elderly individuals or couples who have moved to Hope Meadows to serve as tutors, crossing guards, baby-sitters, playground monitors, and mentors to the children there.

If you ever doubt the power of a Life Brand that promises to add value to the world around it, I encourage you to visit Hope Meadows and see what Brenda Eheart's transcending vision has inspired. She has been invited to the White House and to testify before the U.S. Congress. Her creation has been featured in national news stories and honored by dozens of organizations. Brenda could have no greater reward than the happy and confident looks on the faces of the children who ride bicycles, walk to school, and play on the sidewalks of Hope Meadows.

She and people like her are my benchmarks for success. It's not what you have at the end of life, it's what you leave behind that matters. She has been invited to take the model of Hope Meadows and spread it around the world, to help other children find a foundation of love and support so that they can make their own contributions to society as adults. The legacy of Brenda's Life Brand will be felt for many generations.

## THE CREATION OF MY LIFE BRAND

In my previous book, *You Can Make It Happen,* I offered readers the Success Process that I discovered relatively late in my life. I'd been a good athlete, playing basketball through high school, then college, and in Europe for a few years. Then I had drifted into a career in criminal justice, working my way up into an administrative post in the federal prison system. Later, I moved into public relations and marketing. By my mid-thirties, I was doing very well by most standards, but I was just coasting along. It's not that I wasn't working hard. It's just that I wasn't in control of my life. I didn't have a plan or a process for achieving my goals and dreams. Then, through my business contacts, I began to meet some of the most successful people in the world: entrepreneurs, community activists, government leaders, artists, entertainers, dynamic men and women from all walks of life. They were all very different people, but in talking with them, I began to see that each one of their lives had followed a similar pattern.

I want to make it clear that these people were all successful in their own ways. Not all of them were famous or rich, but they all felt good about what they were doing and how they were living their lives. And most of them had worked very hard to get what they wanted from life. I was intrigued by their focus, drive, and determination.

Up to that point, I had taken life as it came to me. These people had envisioned the lives they wanted and created them. Oprah was really the first person I'd met who had done that. She was just getting started on her dream when we first met, and although she has accomplished a lot—okay, she's done incredibly well—she is *still* working on her brand.

I'm sure you are familiar with her story, so I don't need to repeat it all again here. It's enough to note that she came from an extremely difficult background. Nothing was handed to her. Like most of us, she made mistakes and suffered setbacks. She also suffered some truly terrible things, though she never gave up on her dreams. She believed in herself. I admired her for that. In our years together, I've also witnessed her grow from a successful local television personality, whose life was still pretty much determined by outside influences, into a multimillionaire businesswoman who has seized control of her own destiny and reaped incredible rewards.

While Oprah may not have thought about herself as a brand in the early days, she is very focused on managing, expanding, and protecting her brand today. When other talk show hosts began moving into trash television, it didn't take Oprah long to realize that following that path could destroy the brand she had worked so hard to build. So she headed off in the opposite direction. She started a book club to encourage reading and mental growth. She also focused on topics and guests who could help people improve their physical and spiritual lives. As a result, her brand became stronger than ever. It is now carried on a wide variety of businesses, including companies involved in television and movie production, a book club, a charitable scholarship fund, Internet and cable network ventures, and a magazine.

"Although some companies spend decades trying to build and maintain the trust of their customers, Oprah Winfrey has, in less than 15 years, carefully transformed her international talk show celebrity status into corporate-like stature," noted a *Chicago Tribune* writer in a story headlined BRAND OPRAH.

Most observers see Oprah's business accomplishments. I've witnessed the personal and spiritual development she's undergone. In talking to other successful people, I came to see a similar pattern or process that they followed, consciously or unconsciously, in pursuit of their dreams. I charted that process as a Nine-Step Plan for Success and wrote about it in *You Can Make It Happen.* Here is a quick review of those steps:

### Step 1: Check Your ID
Before you decide what you want for your life, you first must understand who you are, what the influences are on your life, and why you act and think the way you do.

### Step 2: Create Your Vision
To seek a better life, you first have to decide what you want by setting realistic goals for your family and personal relationships, your job or career, and your role in your community.

### Step 3: Develop Your Travel Plan
Once your goals are set, the next step is to develop a plan to go after those goals, but it must be consistent with the values and principles that you've chosen to guide your life.

### Step 4: Master the Rules of the Road
When driving on the highway, you have to follow the rules of the road in order to reach your destination safely; the same holds true when pursuing your life goals. There will be distractions and disappointments, but by learning how to stay focused and self-motivated you can stay on track.

### Step 5: Step into the Outer Limits
In order to reach your goals, you are going to have to push yourself and take risks that move you beyond your comfort zone. This step teaches you how to take well-calculated risks

and how to find the courage to push yourself into those outer limits where you can grow and thrive.

### Step 6: Pilot the Seasons of Change

To change the results you have been getting in life, you have to change your approach. That may mean changing the people you hang out with, changing the place you live, or changing your attitude. It is impossible to move ahead without leaving something behind, and in this step you learn how to handle the stages of positive change.

### Step 7: Build Your Dream Team

I don't know anyone who has achieved success without help along the way. Building supportive relationships and learning how to be both trustworthy and trusting is a key element in the Success Process.

### Step 8: Win by a Decision

Making the right decisions is crucial to building a successful life. There is a process for evaluating decisions, and in this step you learn how.

### Step 9: Commit to Your Vision

Having a commitment to your goals involves devoting your time and energy to the pursuit of your vision and making it a top priority in your life. Most people have dreams; the secret is learning to transform dreams into realistic goals and committing to them.

Originally, I had no thoughts of sharing this process with other people in a book. I did it for myself. I was trying to get out of a rut, and to tell you the truth, I was also struggling to get out from under Oprah's shadow. It was tough being constantly identified as "Oprah's boyfriend." I had a powerful need to establish my own identity. As an athlete, I had a lot of pride in my own accomplishments and, for a while, I felt that people didn't see the value that I brought to the table as a businessperson. Nobody wants his or her identity to be based solely on whom they date or whom they are married to. The "boyfriend" thing drove me crazy early on, but looking back, it was one of the best things that ever happened to me because, for the first time in my adult life, it got me focused on setting my own goals and aggressively pursuing them.

After I identified the Success Process, I became more and more excited about it. I realized I needed to create a structure to keep myself on track. When I began following the step-by-step process and pursuing my goals, incredible things happened in my life. Slowly, I began building my core business, and then, more rapidly, other businesses and opportunities began to open up for me. If you believe the definition of *lucky* that says it is "being prepared for opportunity," then I am a lucky guy. I prepared myself by following the Success Process, and when the opportunities came my way, I was ready.

Today, I am the CEO of S. Graham & Associates, an educational company that creates customized corporate-training and leadership-development programs, products, and services.

Along with owning those businesses, I am the author of four books, an adjunct professor at Northwestern University's Kellogg Graduate School of Management, visiting professor at The George Washington University, distinguished visiting professor at Coker College, and the founder and chairman of the nonprofit Leadership Institute of Chicago. I also serve on the national boards of a number of other nonprofit groups, including Junior Achievement and the Children's Scholarship Fund, established by two outstanding entrepreneurs, Ted Forstmann, the former chairman of Gulfstream Aerospace, and John Walton, director of Wal-Mart Stores Inc., to expand educational opportunities for children from low-income families.

I am living my dreams, and because I have a successful and active professional life, my relationships are stronger than ever before. I no longer worry about what other people say or write about me. Of course, I'm still growing and learning, setting new goals for myself and going after them.

In fact, one of my observations about the ongoing process of success led to the creation of this book. As I began to build my own businesses and create opportunities for myself, it became increasingly apparent to me that I had unknowingly become "a brand" in the marketplace. Without even thinking about changing my brand identity, I had done it.

It really hit me that I had become a "brand" when business leaders, entrepreneurs, and philanthropists whom I respected began inviting me to do business with them or to otherwise participate in their companies, projects, and charities. Observing that, it dawned on me—I could help other people transcend the narrow inner world of "self-help" by teaching them to develop a much more fulfilling *value* mentality through the creation of Life Brands.

## THE POWER OF A QUALITY LIFE BRAND

I've discovered that when you work to build on your strengths by developing your talents and expanding your knowledge to create a well-defined Life Brand, the world opens up to you. Your career blossoms. Your relationships become stronger. Your value in the community becomes more widely recognized. When you become actively engaged in managing your brand by offering value to the world around you, other people begin to perceive you differently. They see you are committed to something more than your own success, and they buy into your dreams too. Others begin to see that you believe in your own value and that in associating with you their value will also increase.

Once you have gone through the Nine-Step Plan for Success and put yourself on track to your dreams, whatever they are, then you certainly should do all that you can to create, manage, and expand your Life Brand. Why? Well, there are two important reasons. The first is that managing your brand allows you to continue to grow as a person. The second is that if you don't manage your brand, you can very easily lose your focus and fall back into the trap of letting life sweep you along. It is also easy to lose focus if you don't have a good sense of what you want your brand to represent and how you want to expand it.

In this book, I am going to show you how to move to the next level in the Success Process by doing just that. Before we get started, I'd like you to get a pen and paper and write down what each of the following names means to you:

1. Nelson Mandela
2. Fidel Castro
3. Dennis Rodman
4. Sammy Sosa
5. Albert Belle
6. Michael Jordan

7. Ralph Lauren
8. Martha Stewart
9. Stephen Covey
10. Oprah Winfrey

Obviously, these are all famous people, but each of them has a unique public image, or *brand*. Even those who are involved in the same field—like baseball stars Sammy Sosa and Albert Belle, basketball's Michael Jordan and Dennis Rodman, political leaders Nelson Mandela and Fidel Castro, and fashion's Ralph Lauren and Martha Stewart—have very different brands, don't they?

It's also interesting how each of these people has managed his or her brand differently. Dennis Rodman, for example, has done all he can to cultivate an image of blue-collar determination along with rebelliousness and defiance. His former teammate Michael Jordan, on the other hand, has a carefully protected image of integrity, teamwork, and the highest level of performance. I'm not asking you to judge either man. Each has been successful in his own way. Neither of them is perfect. Think about their brands and what they represent, and then ask yourself which one of them will have more opportunities and the greatest success *over the long term* if they maintain the same brand identities.

As we begin putting your Life Brand together in the chapters that follow, I'd like you to keep in mind that this is a long-term process. It's a life's work. It's the most important project you will undertake. It's your path and your legacy. The thought and care you put into building your Life Brand will help determine how great a mark you make on this world.

## WHAT WILL YOUR LEGACY BE?

One of the greatest Life Brands of our generation, Nelson Mandela, became well known as a prominent foe of apartheid in his native country, South Africa. He was imprisoned for his beliefs, but for more than twenty-seven years he continued to fight from behind bars for the freedom of his fellow blacks in South Africa. When he was released from prison, he was elected president of his country, and he is now hailed around the world as a champion of freedom.

Nelson Mandela and many of the other people on the preceding list have created brands that enable them to keep expanding their influence far beyond their original bases, don't they? Why is that? How do they keep expanding their influence year after year? Why does it work for some people on the list and not for others?

What have they got that you don't have? *Absolutely nothing!* What's that? You say you came from a background of poverty, so you don't have the same opportunities? I'm afraid that's no excuse. Look at that list again. I can name several people on it who were born into poverty but rose above it. Many of them felt at one time or another in their lives that they had no talents, limited opportunities, and huge obstacles to overcome. You are not alone in that. But if you follow the Success Process and take responsibility for creating and managing your own Life Brand, I guarantee that you will move much closer to your goals and dreams. It doesn't matter who you are or where you came from, you too have the opportunity to contribute your gifts and create a life of value. Nelson Mandela was imprisoned for more than twenty-seven years, yet he persevered because he took a stand and never lost sight of his vision for a better nation. Nelson Mandela vowed that no matter what his jailers did to him physically, they would never defeat his spirit. They could lock him up. They could beat him. But they could not overcome his powerful belief in himself, nor could they enslave his mind. And he was right!

When those who imprisoned him were finally forced by world opinion to set Nelson Mandela free, the power of his spirit liberated an entire nation, and it inspired the world! What gave him such power over his circumstances? What can you do to build your internal capacity and make yourselves *that* strong?

What if Mandela had turned to his jailers one day and said, "You know what? I'm sick of being locked in this cell. I'm sick of eating gruel. I'm sick of being cold and lonely. I want a cheeseburger. I want to see my family. So, tell you what. I'm going to make an announcement that it's okay to let other people tell you where you can live, where you have to work, and where you can go every minute of every day of your lives. Then you can let me go, right?"

Now, if Mandela had done that, what would his brand stand for today? Would he be considered a great man? Would he have the ability to inspire and influence millions of people? Of course not. What makes him such a great man is that he *stands* for something. He believed that one man could change the world, and he did it by consistently demonstrating the values and principles that we associate with courageous leaders.

Mandela is an ordinary man with an extraordinary brand. You have that same power within you. As long as you are willing to stand for something. As long as you remain consistent. As long as you refuse to allow your circumstances to blind you to your opportunities!

# Lessons from the Brand Styles of the Rich and Famous

CHAPTER THREE

> Every human being is a brand. The way you socialize, who you
> know, what you say. I just had the good fortune of being in this
> culture where there is a market for nice, funny guys.

THAT QUOTE ON personal branding comes from a source that might surprise you. I found it in a *Forbes* magazine interview with comedian Jerry Seinfeld. The writer of the story called him "the purest comedy brand in showbiz" and "(maybe) the purest brand in entertainment."

"The purest brand"—what does that mean? When you hear Jerry Seinfeld's name, what do you think of? What does his brand promise? What do you get when you buy into Jerry Seinfeld?

You get humor and laughter. Seinfeld is a comedian pure and simple. He is not a dramatic actor, nor is he a song and dance man. He's *purely* funny. Unlike most other comedians who have become television stars—Bill Cosby, Drew Carey, and Tim Allen, to name a few—Seinfeld played *himself* on his show. As a result, when most people think of Jerry Seinfeld, they get a clear picture of a comedian.

As a celebrity brand, Seinfeld's promise is entertainment. People believe they will be entertained if Seinfeld appears on a show, in a commercial, or at a nightclub. The value of his *celebrity brand* is clear-cut. He offers quality comedy in the same way that the Disney product brand represents a promise of quality family entertainment or the Dockers product brand represents a promise of comfortable casual slacks.

When Seinfeld was developing his television sitcom concept in 1989, he was popular on the talk show circuit and in clubs but he didn't have a great deal of clout in the entertainment industry. Still, he was adamant that if he was going to have a television show, he wanted to play himself—not a teacher, not a social worker; a comedian. He'd become very successful as a stand-up comic and he didn't want to do anything that might confuse people who had bought into his brand. He chose to stick with the talent that had taken him to that point. He kept it pure and consistent and he reaped incredible rewards by building on what he does best.

As a result of his strong brand, Seinfeld was able to retire from his television show in May 1998 knowing that his celebrity status would not be diminished, nor would his income. At that point, the show was already producing $2 billion in syndication revenues, which paid him more than $267 million, according to *Forbes*.

## CELEBRITIES ARE BRAND MASTERS

To help further your understanding of the value of building a Life Brand, I want to take you on a trip to the land of the celebrity brand. A celebrity is a widely recognized, high-profile individual whose name (or brand) has the ability to draw attention and add value to whatever it is associated with.

A celebrity in any field generally has greater opportunities to generate income, to reach a wide audience, and to have a bigger impact than those who do not stand out.

One of the primary benefits of building a Life Brand is that it helps you clearly define your goals and the value you represent through your unique blend of talents, knowledge, and personal characteristics. While the goals of a celebrity brand are generally more limited than those of a Life Brand, celebrity brands offer great examples of many of the principles of personal branding.

As you read this chapter, think about how you might apply celebrity branding techniques to the development of your Life Brand.

While the concept of branding has its origins in the marketing of consumer products, the branding of celebrities was developed decades ago by the studio star-making machines of Hollywood. The studio image-makers would take in aspiring young actors and actresses like Archibald Leach, Issur Danielovitch, Sophia Scicolone, and Norma Jean Mortenson and create entirely new identities for them in order to transform them into bigger-than-life Hollywood idols, complete with movie marquee names. Archie Leach became Cary Grant. Issur Danielovitch was reborn as Kirk Douglas. Sophia Scicolone became Sophia Loren, and plain old Norma Jean Mortenson was transfigured into Marilyn Monroe.

While some of that creative image-making still goes on today, Hollywood's celebrity branding campaigns now are geared more toward extending the careers and increasing the earning power of the stars. Celebrity branding is a big business, and it isn't restricted just to people in the entertainment industry. I find it interesting that ordinary people are also becoming masters of the techniques of celebrity brand management. As a result, many of them have stretched and increased considerably their earning potential as well as their influence.

## THE POWER OF A CELEBRITY BRAND EXTENDS TO ALL WALKS OF LIFE

I am thinking in particular of a person who was a county prosecutor, which is one of the lower-paying, lower-profile jobs in the legal profession. Before she was selected to be part of the prosecution team in the O.J. Simpson trial, Marcia Clark was a little-known county employee. When she went to trial against a celebrity client represented by highly paid celebrity lawyers, she was swept up in the media spotlight. She did not waste the opportunity.

Do you remember how she was initially portrayed in the media at the start of the trial? She was described as driven, no-nonsense, and tough-minded. Photographs from the early days of the trial show a woman with a very practical "perm" hairstyle, little makeup, and conservative business clothing. Her image changed dramatically as the trial progressed. She had her hair styled in a more feminine, trendy look similar to that worn by the women television reporters who were covering the trial. She also began wearing designer dresses and suits as well as more flattering makeup.

It was a dramatic transformation, and it worked. Legal experts will argue for years over whether the prosecution did a good job in the O.J. Simpson trial, but there is no doubt that Marcia Clark's brand came out ahead. After the trial, she was a full-blown celebrity with a $4.5 million book contract, invitations to all of the major celebrity events, and, eventually, her own show on Court TV. The point is that Marcia Clark took control of her situation instead of letting it control her. If she had not made the effort to "brand" herself, she might still be working as a county prosecutor. Instead, she took responsibility and control and expanded her earning power and her influence by building a celebrity brand.

## GETTING YOUR MESSAGE THROUGH ALL THE NOISE

For Marcia Clark and other noncelebrities who become swept up in the spotlight for one reason or another, the next challenge is to keep building and expanding the celebrity brand so that they have *staying power.* That is the mark of the strongest brands, whether you are talking about products on the shelf, celebrities in the tabloids, or a young software designer trying to make a name for himself in the Silicon Valley. Everyone wants to be a star in these times because having a high profile is the best way to get your message through all of the clamor and clutter of the modern world.

The Tower of Babel still babbles on. It blares at us in a relentless barrage of multimedia, including television, radio, e-mail, cellular phones, fax machines, billboards, magazines, newspapers, and movie screens. That leaves us with two problems. The first is, how do we shut out all that noise? The second is, how do we get our *own* messages through? How do you stand out from the crowd? If you are a lawyer, corporate leader, real estate developer, therapist, designer, marketing executive, chef, security consultant, or personal fitness trainer, how do let your *target markets* know about your unique talents, skills, knowledge, and character?

You develop a celebrity brand. "Being a celebrity expands your commercial possibilities," said Jerry Seinfeld, who is so into brand consciousness that he considered starting an advertising agency.

The commercial value of creating a celebrity brand certainly has not been lost on businessmen like Donald Trump and Richard Branson of Virgin Airlines. They are among the most successful celebrity-branded business executives in a crowded field. They've cashed in by becoming high-profile "stars" in their respective arenas and then stretched their brands into other areas. Trump was a New York commercial developer who cultivated an image of business savvy, affluence, and success, even in those times when he was nearly bankrupt. He has ridden his celebrity brand through hard times and back. His holdings have grown to include not just office buildings in Manhattan but hotels, casinos, and, at one point, his own airline.

Richard Branson may be the reigning king of celebrity business brands. He cultivates an image as a jet-setting, free-spirited entrepreneur and uses his celebrity brand to market his music store as well as his airline, broadcast stations, television programs, and soft drinks. He has been known to dress up as Spiderman or descend from a hot-air balloon at the openings of his Virgin Records stores. "For Branson, high visibility is a strategic tool that has made his personality inseparable from his products," note Irving Rein, Philip Kotler, and Martin Stoller, the authors of *High Visibility: The Making and Marketing of Professionals into Celebrities.*

## THE CELEBRITY BRAND BANDWAGON

These businessmen are not alone in trading on celebrity brands. Butcher, baker, or investment portfolio maker? Tailor, tinker, soldier, spy? You name a trade or a calling and the odds are strong that there's someone who stands out with a celebrity brand.

☛BUTCHER?  How about a celebrity-brand hamburger-chain owner? Dave Thomas turned his Wendy's restaurants into a major player in the supercompetitive fast-food franchise business by developing a brand that regular folks can identify with. Instead of hiring a professional actor to pitch his burgers, Thomas stepped in and did it himself. His down-to-earth personality has helped Wendy's climb to the top of the heap.

☛BAKER?  Top chefs are no longer content to stay in the kitchen. They have become masters of building celebrity brands and extending their reach. Wolfgang Puck. Julia Child. Emeril Lagasse. Rick Bayless. Charlie Trotter. These high-profile celebrity-brand chefs own restaurants, write best-selling cookbooks, host television shows, and sell their own brands of frozen foods, spices, and sauces. Portuguese chef Lagasse, who has a hit television show called *Emeril Live* on the Food Network, told *Forbes* that the key to his success was to back away from the stove and develop a celebrity brand: "Chefs have to step out of the kitchen and become restaurateurs and businessmen. They also have to wear other hats: television, public speaking, dealing with lawyers—it goes on and on."

☞FINANCIAL WIZARDS?    Years ago, playing the stock market was the exclusive domain of the ultrarich, and they certainly didn't share the names of their key financial advisers. Today, investment gurus are among the biggest celebrities on television, on the lecture tours, and as authors. The ever-growing list includes Peter Lynch, Warren Buffett, Elaine Garzarelli, and Motley Fool brothers David and Tom Gardner.

The Gardner brothers began their down-to-earth investment newsletter as a print publication but discovered that the Internet's message boards were a better way to attract more followers. In 1994, they opened the Motley Fool Financial Forum on America Online, and it proved to be so popular that AOL asked them to become a content provider for its readers. Their AOL Forum and Web sites have become enormously popular with both investors and advertisers, spawning a retail operation called FoolMart with a wide range of their Motley Fool brand electronic products, calendars, and other merchandise. They have also written four best-selling investment advice books, started a nationally syndicated newspaper column, and launched a national radio show.

☞SOLDIER?    Retired General Colin Powell was the National Security Adviser to Ronald Reagan and chairman of the Joint Chiefs of Staff under George Bush and Bill Clinton. He is proof that old soldiers never fade away if they create strategic celebrity brands. He first commanded public recognition while serving as the official military spokesman during the Persian Gulf war, but he has expanded his brand—and earned more money (a reported $4.8 million annually) than most generals dream of—by flirting with a run for the presidency, writing a best-selling biography, and cashing in on the lecture circuit. He now serves as secretary of state under President George W. Bush.

☛SPY?    Former CIA agent turned political operative E. Gordon Liddy was one of the villains of the Watergate scandal, but his earnings from book deals, radio shows, and speaking fees are the result of his cloak-and-dagger celebrity brand.

☛EX-MONKS?    Self-help authors Thomas Moore, who wrote the 1992 best-seller *Care of the Soul,* and John Gray, the creator of *Men Are from Mars, Women Are from Venus,* are both former religious leaders who became self-help advisers to millions of people through their celebrity brands. Gray has expanded his brand with ten books, a magazine, and a Mattel board game.

☛EVANGELISTS?    Billy Graham, Pat Robertson, the Reverend Jesse Jackson, Robert Schuller. All of these celebrity-brand clergymen have built huge congregations and influenced millions of people because of the power of their highly visible brands.

☛LAWYERS?    Johnnie Cochran, Alan Dershowitz, F. Lee Bailey, Marcia Clark, et al. In a profession packed with powerful figures, it is the celebrity brands who win no matter what the jury decides. Cochran may well be the leading celebrity-brand attorney, with two books, a movie deal, a television show, lectures, and—the ultimate mark of celebrity status—a *Saturday Night Live* actor who has become famous for imitating him.

☞FITNESS INSTRUCTORS?    Most of them work either in health clubs or as consultants. Many earn less than $20 an hour, although those who cater to a wealthier clientele can make several hundred thousand dollars a year in places like Beverly Hills; Scottsdale, Arizona; and West Palm Beach, Florida. Nobody in their trade has muscle like the celebrity-brand fitness instructors.

Tae-Bo guru Billy Blanks is one of the latest in a long line that includes the buff and not so buff; from Jane Fonda and Richard Simmons to Suzanne Somers and Charles Atlas. One of the most enduringly successful is both a product and a master of the celebrity branding game. Back in the late seventies, Jake Steinfeld was a young guy who retired from competitive bodybuilding because he didn't believe in taking steroids. He had tried to break into the acting business, but at that point his biggest role was portraying the Incredible Hulk for tourists on the Universal Studios tour.

Jake's career as a fitness instructor to the stars began when an actress friend asked him to help her get in shape for a role. Word got around Hollywood that Jake was discreet, knowledgeable, and a great motivator. He wisely created an air of exclusivity by keeping his telephone number unlisted so that even stars had to know somebody to get on his client list. Within a remarkably short time, his Body by Jake celebrity brand was on his own television show, his own fitness network, and several books, and currently includes an entire line of fitness products sold on infomercials, the Internet, and the Home Shopping Network.

Jake Steinfeld is now a multimillionaire entrepreneur with a powerful celebrity brand. It's interesting that Jake's career really took off, and his celebrity brand was established, when he developed a business that helped celebrities improve *their* brand images.

## THE CELEBRITY BRANDING INDUSTRY

Because of the successes of celebrity brands in a wide range of fields, an entire support industry has flourished. It includes agents, personal managers, ghostwriters, lawyers, accountants, acting coaches, speech writers, voice coaches, public relations experts, business managers, publicists, travel facilitators, diet consultants, dressing consultants, image designers, charity coordinators, plastic surgeons, hairdressers, and psychiatrists.

It's said that NBA star Shaquille O'Neal has so many people helping build his celebrity brand that they hold regular, two-day "Shaq Summits" to keep everyone on the team informed. Like most athletes, Shaq has reaped rewards from another benefit of the celebrity brand—product endorsements. Top celebrity-brand athletes can expect to earn three times as much from endorsements as they make on the playing field. Andre Agassi, who is a spokesman for Nike and Canon, among other products, reportedly earns $11 million a year, with only $1 million of that coming directly from earnings on the court.

The biggest brand-name companies are willing to pay enormous amounts of money for brand-name celebrity endorsements. Nike alone once had an annual budget of $300 million just to pay celebrity-brand athletes for endorsing its footwear. Its number-one spokesman, Michael Jordan, was reportedly earning $69 million a year even *after* he'd retired from basketball, thanks to all his product-endorsement deals.

Phil Quartarao, president of Warner Bros. Records, told *Forbes* that today's real stars are the ones, like Michael, who can create an image above and beyond their medium: "Michael is not promoting a song or a movie, he's promoting an image. That's what stardom is all about."

## Celebrity Brands Just Keep Going and Going and Going

Celebrities are acutely aware of the need to develop, market, and stretch their talents. They are fiercely protective of their brands. They are always analyzing their markets and looking for ways to expand their audience. So, if you are seeking role models who can teach you how to use branding as a method for creating opportunities, there are many great examples out there.

Seinfeld, in particular, is acutely aware of the power of his celebrity brand. He and other brand-conscious public figures are like a huge family of Energizer Bunnies. They just keep going and going as their brands keep growing and growing. They become celebrities in one arena and then extend their reach, and their careers, by expanding their brands into other fields with books, movies, product endorsements, commercials, and even entire new careers as entrepreneurs and politicians.

If this doesn't seem unusual to you, then you may not be familiar with the way things used to work for most celebrities. In the past, they were more like Halley's Comet. They'd appear on the horizon, brilliant and irresistible to look at, but they burned fast and furious, often disappearing entirely from view after a few short years. Not so long ago, an actor was con-

sidered versatile if he could dance and sing too. Celebrity athletes, for example, often found that their options were very
limited after the conclusion of their playing careers. Jesse
Owens was perhaps the most famous athlete in the world after
destroying Hitler's claims to Aryan supremacy at the 1936
Olympics in Berlin. Yet Jesse simply was not able to extend and
expand his brand on the same massive scale as today's
Olympic and sports heroes who land book deals, win movie
roles, go on national promotional tours, and become major
players in other fields of endeavor.

There were exceptions, of course, and some of them
could be considered prototypes for today's brand-conscious
celebrities. Johnny Weissmuller was a dominant Olympic
champion swimmer in the 1920s. After winning five gold
medals he went on to considerable success as an actor, making
twelve Tarzan movies and sixteen more films as Jungle Jim, a
role he later took to television.

Another actor of that era, Ronald Reagan, certainly knew
a bit about building and managing his personal brand. After
making fifty films, Reagan saw in the 1950s that his acting career appeared to be fading, so he redirected his energies and
considerable charisma into a high-profile role as a spokesman
and television host for General Electric. Then, in the mid-
1960s, he began a political career that carried him from the
California governor's mansion to the White House, where
he was one of the most popular presidents in history. Even
his detractors admired the powerful personal brand of integrity and patriotism he created. Reagan is as celebrated
today for his image-making skills as for his accomplishments
as a leader.

Celebrities have become masterful, aggressive branding
wizards, and so to help you get started in creating your Life

Brand, I've identified important lessons you can learn from the branding styles of the rich and famous.

# FIVE KEY LESSONS FROM CELEBRITY BRANDS

## Lesson One: *Value* + *Brand Recognition* = *Success*

It used to be that some people were famous for being famous. They didn't actually *do* anything of note. You don't see much of that anymore. Those do-nothing people don't last in the world of celebrity brands, where the most powerful players are those who know they must bring value to the table and keep adding to it all the time. The biggest television, movie, book, and endorsement contracts go to the stars who have built up a loyal audience because they deliver on their promises to entertain them. They can virtually guarantee that audience to the networks, producers, and advertisers who pay for their services.

I don't know many comedians, but I'd be willing to bet there aren't a lot of them who earn hundreds of millions of dollars each year. The difference between the earnings of a comedian doing stand-up at the local comedy club for a few hundred dollars a night and the multimillionaire Seinfeld is not just directly related to the quality of their jokes but also to the strength of their brands.

In a world of fifteen-second sound bytes and fifteen minutes of fame, celebrities are especially aware of the importance of always working to increase their brand value. Simply being well known can be an asset if you know how to manage your brand and maintain a high profile over the years. There are a great many retired athletes who are still earning good incomes from product endorsements, public appearances, and even autograph and licensing deals because they still have strong name recognition.

But being famous, recognized, or in a position of high visibility is not enough for most celebrities to build long-term personal brands. They must have control of their brand images and they must then manage them thoughtfully.

*The lesson for the Life Brand builder is that it's not enough to simply market yourself as a brand; you must build value into your brand too, and you must manage it thoughtfully to keep your visibility high and your image positive.*

## Lesson No. 2: *Powerful Brands Rub Off*

Seinfeld's celebrity brand is so powerful that his former girlfriend, Shoshanna Lonstein, won national media attention and $1 million in sales upon introducing her own line of lingerie more than a year *after* their relationship had ended. The other actors who appeared on Seinfeld's show benefited from their association with him too. Most of them were not well known until they became part of the *Seinfeld* cast. Their celebrity brands grew to extraordinary value as a result. Even a New York City deli that was the model for the "Soup Nazi's" deli on *Seinfeld* became a major tourist attraction because of its association with the show.

That's the mark of a powerful brand—whether it is a product brand, a celebrity brand, or a personal Life Brand—it adds value to everything and everyone associated with it. When Oprah recommends a book, praises a movie, or features someone on her show, each benefits from heightened visibility. Her endorsements have helped dozens of authors become celebrity brands themselves, just as Michael Jordan's endorsement helped Nike become the leader in athletic footwear. In the same way, Quincy Jones, who helped Michael Jackson establish himself as a solo act, has launched the careers of many young performers, including Brandy, by including them in his concept albums and live performance events.

*Keep this lesson in mind when you are building and managing your Life Brand. Always strive to associate with other strong Life Brands who can add value and visibility to yours.*

### Lesson No. 3: *Don't Be Afraid to Stretch Your Brand*

Do you remember when a folk singer was a folk singer, and not a multimedia conglomerate? When a professional wrestler couldn't get elected dog catcher? When a basketball star kept his game on the court? Those days appear to be well over. Today's celebrities are relentless in stretching their brands to reach as wide a target market as possible while keeping their careers alive for years and years.

○ Jewel Kilcher's first folk-rock album in 1995 sold 10 million copies and, as a result, she became a huge star. Because of the strength of her celebrity brand, she was offered a $2 million deal to publish her book of poems. There are very few poets who attract that kind of book advance—"starving" and "poet" have long been considered companion terms. Jewel's first book of poetry sold more than 500,000 copies and became a best-seller. She is now expanding her brand into acting.

o Jesse "The Body" Ventura became a celebrity brand as a professional wrestler. He used his notoriety as a platform to run first for mayor, then for governor of Minnesota. After winning the governor's seat, he pinned down his own $500,000 book deal, and a movie deal too. He also began licensing products bearing his brand, including a line of action figures resembling him as the governor, the Navy SEAL, and the wrestler.

o Shaquille O'Neal has stretched his celebrity brand from the basketball court to the recording studio (five rap albums), movie studios (*Shazaam, Steel,* and *Blue Chip*), and corporate America, where he has more than $10 million in product endorsement and licensing agreements, including the Shaq Fu video games.

o Martha Stewart serves as a multiple-threat celebrity-brand model. After obtaining celebrity-brand status through her television appearances, she formed a multimedia company to produce her own television and radio shows. She also has a syndicated newspaper column, a magazine, and has written nearly thirty books. She licenses the Martha Stewart brand name for products ranging from gardening tools to house paint, which have sales of nearly $1 billion annually. In the fall of 1999, she leveraged that brand power into more than $1 billion by taking her company public and setting a record for an initial public stock offering.

o Pop singer Brandy first appeared on the celebrity-brand screen with a guest appearance on an album produced by Quincy Jones. Since then she has sold 8 million of her own records, starred in a television sitcom, and landed a $1.5 million modeling contract.

Look through that list again and consider what brand recognition has done for the celebrities I've named. Jesse Ventura probably couldn't take a pounding in the ring anymore, but his brand is still worth $500,000 to a book publisher. Colin Powell has retired from the military, but his public profile continues to be high and his speaking fees are near the top.

They aren't alone in increasing their value through brand marketing, of course. Michael Jordan will *probably* (you can never say "never" with him) never play in another NBA game, but his powerful brand will keep bringing him millions and millions of dollars a year through product endorsements, commercials, and other deals. Even "stars" who may not have much time in the limelight can build incredible wealth by moving quickly to extend their brands. The Spice Girls singing group grossed $65 million in 1998, but less than half that came from music sales. They earned $35 million from their movie, books, and other merchandise.

*If you build real value into your Life Brand, there is no reason to fear stretching and trying your talents and testing your knowledge in new areas.*

## Lesson No. 4:
### *Strong Brands Can Withstand Challenges and Mistakes*

Strong brands survive. Cindy Crawford has had considerable success moving from her high-profile position as a fashion supermodel into product endorsements for Revlon, workout videos, books, calendars, and scores of other Cindy-brand products. She also did well as the host of *House of Style,* a fashion show on MTV, but Cindy has been less successful in her attempts to launch an acting career. Her performance in her 1995 movie debut, *Fair Game,* was widely panned, but that has not appeared to damage her high-powered brand. Even though she is well beyond the age once considered past prime for supermodels, Cindy's brand appears to be stronger than ever. Her recent pregnancy and the birth of her first child have not appeared to slow her down at all. The new mother has lucrative spokesmodel deals with Ellen Tracy and Omega watches, as well as a three-year contract to appear on ABC's programs.

*People* magazine may well be the Bible for celebrity brands. Here's what it has to say about Cindy's: "What do you call a supermodel who outdoes all the other supermodels? Ubermodel? Megamodel? Modelgrande? Supermodels by definition have parlayed magazine-cover and runway success into mini-industries, but the only thing mini about Crawford is her skirts. In addition to producing the requisite exercise videos, swimsuit calendar and beauty book, Crawford has wrested movie deals from Hollywood and, in 1997, a three-year contract with ABC that will enable the network to sprinkle her famous face across its schedule, from sportscasts to *Good Morning America.* All that, and Crawford—despite the passing of her prime modeling days—still sells magazines like nobody else."

If they have built their brands carefully and thoughtfully, like Cindy Crawford, celebrities can afford to handle challenges that threaten their brand images. Oprah was sued by Texas cattlemen who felt she had disparaged the eating of meat on her show. The long trial could have been a disastrous public relations problem—if Oprah had not handled it so wisely. She took her entire show to Texas during the trial so that her fans would not be shortchanged and, in the process, won the heart of the Lone Star State.

*A strong brand that offers lasting value can weather storms, bounce back from failures, and survive challenges.*

## Lesson No. 5:
### *It Pays to Monitor Your Markets and Adjust Your Brand*

While other pop singers of the 1980s have come and gone, Madonna, a skilled manager of her celebrity brand, is still with us. She has read and mirrored changes in popular culture and transformed her image from pop star to rebellious temptress to earth mother, reaping millions along the way in record and ticket sales, movies, merchandising, and books. She has now leveraged her celebrity brand into more permanent power with a $50 million investment that has made her a part-owner in Maverick Recording Company. Madonna's likely role model is probably another one-name wonder woman, Cher, the 1960s pop star turned 1970s television star turned 1980s movie star, who is undergoing a 1990s resurgence as a pop star.

Both Cher and Madonna have been controversial. Both have angered conservatives at one time or another with their style of dress and their lifestyles in general. But both have made thoughtful adjustments to keep their celebrity brands alive. They've carefully monitored changes in tastes and culture and adjusted their images as their markets have changed. Just as it has appeared they might have outlived their welcome, these two canny celebrity brands always seem to reinvent themselves.

*You can never take your target market for granted. You should be alert to changing tastes and needs and be prepared to make adjustments to ensure that your brand is always offering something of value.*

## LIFE BRANDS VERSUS A CELEBRITY BRAND

Celebrity brands are fun to observe because, in most cases, their mission is simple and it's easy to see how they are maneuvering to extend their careers as long as possible. People often envy celebrities for all the apparent glamor and trappings of fame that they enjoy. In truth, there is a great deal of hard work involved in maintaining the value of a celebrity brand. It's much more difficult to maintain a high public profile constantly, and to develop new projects that exceed or match those that they've done before. The pressure is tremendous—and the failure rate can be high.

The good news is that while there are lessons you can learn from studying the brand-building skills of celebrities, the task of building, maintaining, and stretching a Life Brand is different in many ways. The competition may not be as intense. The pressure to stay in the spotlight is not nearly as great, but creating a Life Brand has many of the same benefits.

You and I may not need public acclaim to keep our careers alive or to make us feel fulfilled. Most of us do want to build Life Brands that offer value in the workplace, in our relationships, and in the community over our lifetimes. In the next chapter, we're going to start building your personal, quality brand by looking at what value, or equity, you bring to the table.

# Brand Value with a Capital *You!*

## CHAPTER FOUR

> Try not to become a man of success, but rather a man of value.
>
> —ALBERT EINSTEIN

**I WALKED INTO** a friend's office recently and my eyes were drawn to a colorful poster on his wall. It was a collage of photographs and words cut from newspapers. My friend's nine-year-old daughter, Jessica, had created the poster. At the top of it, she'd written in pencil, "All about me."

The pictures and cut-out words all represented something from Jessica's life. There were promotional photographs of her favorite movies (*A Bug's Life, The Waterboy,* and *The RugRats*), a picture of her favorite car (a Volkswagen Beetle), and her favorite vacation spot (Florida). She had also pasted on words that represented other aspects of her life (*Dad, Mom, piano, microphone, holidays, home, Drew Barrymore, rings*), her birthday (December 17), and one of her characteristic emotions (*panic!*).

It was a cute collage, and I think it said a lot about this child. At a very young age, Jessica has developed a high level of self-awareness. She has begun to identify the things that make her unique in this world. She even had the awareness and self-confidence to note her tendency to panic.

In looking at Jessica's poster, it occurred to me that this collage was really a child's rudimentary attempt to establish her own Life Brand. Young children tend to see the world as something that fits around them. It's only as they grow older and interact more with others that they begin to understand how they fit in. Jessica is a perceptive young lady because she already has a sense that she is part of a larger world.

The secret to building a powerful Life Brand is to know yourself—to understand what talents, skills, or knowledge gives you value in the world around you. Jessica's collage showed that she has begun to establish her identity or brand in the larger world. She is developing her own unique tastes, perspectives, relationships, and characteristics. She understands there is value in her "brand," and one day, she will learn that others value it too.

## EVALUATING YOUR LIFE BRAND

Jessica's brand identity may be vaguely defined, and not yet completely formed, but it is there. If you talk to her parents and teachers, they'll tell you that her poster offers insight into the value she will one day represent as a person. Her creativity, artistic talents, and interest in the world around her are evident.

What about you? Do you think you have a clearly defined Life Brand? Every individual is recognized by others for the relative value he or she represents. Sometimes others' perceptions of you may vary greatly depending on who is describing you and what their experiences with you have been. One of the primary purposes for developing a Life Brand is that it gives *you* more control over those perceptions.

Just as celebrities and consumer product companies strive to control their public images, as well as the marketing and valuing of their brands, it is important that you thoughtfully control how you are perceived and presented. Why? If you don't take an active role in controlling your image or Life Brand, then you will *lose* control of it to people who will pigeonhole you or stereotype you, or even put you down in order to build themselves up.

Take it from me. Because I had not consciously worked to establish *my* Life Brand when I started dating Oprah, the media took control of my brand. They gave me a label that had nothing to do with my work with young people in the community, or the true value I represented as a businessman and community leader. It's a helpless feeling to see others decide what you represent, but no one is truly helpless. It took a great deal of work to regain control of my Life Brand, but I did it. In many ways, the experience was good for me. It forced me to take a hard look at where I was in life and where I wanted to go. It forced me to take control. I sought out mentors and role models. I formed alliances with individuals and businesses with strong brands of their own. I worked hard to refine my communication skills to get my message across.

You too can take control of your future by working to build a quality Life Brand that reflects your strengths, your values, and your ability to contribute to everything and everyone around you. You'll notice that I wrote "your strengths" and not "your weaknesses." Too often, people trying to decide what to do with their lives take the wrong approach. They focus on building *up* their weaknesses, instead of building *upon* their strengths. If you have a low aptitude for mathematics, there is no sense in spending hours and hours trying to bring your math skills up once you've taken the required courses in school. At best you can hope to attain average math skills anyway. Odds are you wouldn't enjoy a job that required strong math skills because it isn't a passion for you. So, why would you want to invest more time? Why not focus instead on the areas in which you are skilled in order to achieve excellence there?

Where do true happiness and fulfillment lie for you—in being average or in being great at something? People often get stuck on their *can't's* and their *but's* instead of moving ahead on their strengths. I did that after I retired from professional basketball. I spent several years drifting, because whenever I'd consider trying something, I'd think, "No, I don't have the skills for that." I really didn't get going until I tried building on my strengths instead of getting caught up on my weaknesses.

"Most people think they know what they are good at. They are usually wrong," notes management expert Peter Drucker. "More often, people know what they are not good at—and even then more people are wrong than right. And yet, a person can perform only from strength."

To get a feel for what your Life Brand strengths may be, take this quick Life Brand Evaluation Test by answering the questions that follow.

## LIFE BRAND EVALUATION TEST

1. What talents, knowledge, skills, and personal characteristics do you have that add value to the lives of those around you?

   _____

   _____

   _____

2. What *value* do you add to:
   • Your business or employer?

   _____

   _____

   • The daily lives of your family members and those closest to you?

   _____

   _____

   • Each of the communities you belong to, including your coworkers and fellow professionals; the organizations, clubs, and teams you are a member; of your neighbors; and others within your circle of influence?

   _____

   _____

3. What can you do to build on your strengths so that you stand out from other people in your profession, in your relationships, and in your communities?

   _____

   _____

4. Under what conditions do you feel most comfortable and perform best? On a team? Individually? In small

groups? Large groups? With direct supervision? Independently?

_____

_____

5. What do you value most:
   - In your work? *Is money what drives you? Status? Power? Creative opportunities? Recognition? Helping others? Making a contribution?*

   _____

   _____

   - In your relationships? *Companionship? Conversation? Support? Romance? Spirituality? Camaraderie? Shared principles? Commitment?*

   _____

   _____

   - In your community life? *Service to others? Safety? Professional networks? Athletics? Social activities?*

   _____

   _____

6. What is your *core identity,* the way in which you are perceived by your employer and coworkers, your family members, and people in your community of friends, neighbors, and acquaintances?

   _____

   _____

   _____

If you can easily answer each of these questions, then you already have the makings of a strong Life Brand. If you can't, read on and you'll get caught up in a hurry.

## LIFE BRANDS ARE FAR-REACHING

Just as consumer product companies create brand-name products to stand out from all of the "clutter" in the marketplace, you need to build a Life Brand to stand out from the crowd in whatever you do. How does the Disney brand stand out from other amusement parks and other animated movie studios? Their brand represents the highest quality, because Disney's theme parks and animated movies are meticulously done. People expect the same attention to detail when they visit a Disney resort, go on a Disney cruise, or buy a Disney toy. They are willing to pay what is often a higher price for "Disney quality." If they don't get it, they are seriously disappointed. Disney's brand represents high standards, and living up to that brand name is a challenge.

There are other brands that stand out because they offer perhaps a lower level of quality but at a more affordable price. Your local amusement park may not be as big, as meticulously maintained and managed, or as widely known as Disney World, but it's probably a lot less expensive to visit, and more accessible too. The point is that every product, and every person, has brand value of some sort. To help your Life Brand stand out, you should always look for ways to add value to everything you do, whether in your personal relationships, at work, or in your community.

The goals of a Life Brand are multidimensional and holistic. They apply not only to your work or career, but also to your relationships and to your role in the larger world. A celebrity's brand is built upon his or her basic appeal to the large but narrowly defined public marketplace. The purpose of that type of brand is to promote and extend the celebrity's career. A product's brand is also rooted in the basic usefulness of the goods in the public marketplace, whether it's a pair of pants, a cleanser, or a toothpaste. This type of brand is designed purely to enhance its profitability for the manufacturer. Your Life Brand is designed to enhance not only your position in the marketplace (your work or career) but also your relationships and your place in the greater community.

Building a Life Brand helps you focus. It also brings you *into* focus in the eyes of others. If you don't know what your Life Brand is, how is anyone else to know what you stand for? When you establish a brand identity, you are saying, "This is how I can add value. This is what I represent. This is who I am."

## YOUR LIFE BRAND CARRIES A PROMISE OF INHERENT VALUE

Like a celebrity brand or a product brand, your Life Brand carries a guarantee or a promise of inherent value. The brands that endure are those that keep their promise and build upon it. Seinfeld's celebrity brand holds the promise that he will entertain you with his humor. Amazon.com's product brand offers convenient and personalized shopping on the Internet. Your Life Brand's promise is contained in your special blend of talents, skills, knowledge, and other personal characteristics that give you value in the world.

Someone buys into your brand by hiring you, becoming your friend, or asking for your assistance or participation. This person is responding to your brand's promise. When I hire an outside consultant or contractor to do specialized work for my company, it is because I've bought into the promise of his or her brand. That person's friends buy into it for different reasons. To them, it may hold a guarantee that the person is a responsible, friendly, and caring individual who is fun to be around.

## VALUING YOUR BRAND

When I talk about personal branding in my seminars, occasionally someone will say, *I don't have any value. There's nothing special about me.* Usually, with just a few questions, I can help such a person see that is not true. We all have skills we can develop and strengths we can build upon. Too often, I've seen people deny their true talents and follow a path that someone else has carved out for them. I can't understand why anyone would want to live like that. Don't bury your talents. Build upon them.

Everyone wants to stand out in some way. It's not about being competitive or being a show-off, it's simply one of our basic human needs. We all want to be valued, to be appreciated, to be loved. Each of us has assets to offer the world. As you go through the process of identifying, building, and expanding your Life Brand in this book, you are going to see all sorts of ways that your "brand assets" have value. For now, let's look at your three primary "target markets":

1. Your career or work
2. Your relationships
3. Your community

## YOUR BRAND VALUE IN THE WORKPLACE

The merits of having a clearly defined Life Brand may be most obvious in your work and career. After all, your employer or customers pay for the value you represent. You market your brand assets to them. Your career depends on your ability to keep adding to those assets by mastering skills, learning new ones, and continuously building value into your brand. The people who represent the highest value in the workplace, or in their careers, are those who contribute the most. It's difficult to put a price on trust and other personal characteristics such as dependability, honesty, tact, discretion, and good humor.

That is why it's wise for you to understand your value in the workplace and to work at enhancing it throughout your working life. If you are not aware of the value of your brand in a given market—in your division, in your company, or in your industry—then you risk being underpaid, underutilized, and undervalued by those around you. If you don't work at always building more value into your brand as your career progresses, you may find yourself *devalued* by the marketplace.

## MANAGING YOUR BRAND IN
## THE WORLD OF WORK

Think about the most successful, high-profile people you know in your profession. They may or may not be the most skilled, most knowledgeable, or most powerful, but they certainly are the most dedicated to managing their brands. There undoubtedly are many commercial developers in Manhattan who were every bit as knowledgeable and hardworking as Donald Trump, but few have had the opportunities that he has had because of his devotion to managing his brand and maintaining high visibility, which acts as a magnet in his business.

Those who stand out in their professions or workplaces generally are people who do so because they've built the strongest reputations or brands. They also are generally very aware of the value of their brands in the market.

If you don't know the worth of your car when you go to trade it in for a new one, then you risk selling it too cheaply. The same thing can happen if you don't fully understand your own value in your "work" market. To stand out in your work or career, you need to identify your strengths and dedicate yourself to building upon them for as long as you continue to pursue your career. That can be a long time. Men and women are working longer into their lives, in part because people simply live longer, healthier lives now. That's another reason why it is important to create a Life Brand and to manage it thoughtfully. The talents that you identify, develop, and build upon now will only increase in value as you gain more and more experience.

The best way to measure your strengths is to ask for feedback from the people you work with, both those above you and those who work for you. Tell them they can submit their analysis anonymously if they'd like. This can be eye-opening, even painful, but if you get similar responses from all sides, you can assume that it is accurate. It's certain that people will pinpoint your weaknesses, but often they will also identify your strengths. You should concentrate on taking what you naturally do well and getting better and better at it. That's how quality Life Brands are built.

Be aware of the weaknesses and do what you can to eliminate any glaring faults, but focus primarily on building upon your strengths. You may have great natural sales skills, but perhaps you are not so strong in presentation, so a little work in that area could possibly take you up to a much higher level. After all, many people are born with musical aptitude, but it takes focus and a great deal of work to become a great musician. We all have bad habits that can keep us from fully developing our strengths. I am great at planning, for example, but I've got a bad habit of procrastinating. By being aware of that tendency and working to correct it, I've been much more successful in putting my plans into action.

## WORKPLACE VALUE EXERCISE

*Write your answers below for future reference.*

1. What skills, knowledge, experience, and other strengths do you have that would be valued by an employer?
   _____
   _____

2. What can you do to build upon them?
   _____
   _____

3. What bad habits do you have that may be slowing your progress?
   _____
   _____
   _____

4. What can you do to get rid of those bad habits, or at least to counteract them?
   _____
   _____
   _____

5. What valued characteristics—such as leadership, creativity, consensus building, problem solving, or motivational skills—would you bring to an employer?
   _____

_____

_____

6. How can you build upon them?

_____

_____

_____

7. What wider range of experience would benefit your work or career? How can you get more outside experience that will increase your value in the workplace?

_____

_____

_____

## YOUR BRAND VALUE IN RELATIONSHIPS

When you go shopping for clothes, you look for the brands that you value for their style, price, durability, or fit. Similarly, when you go "shopping" for companionship, you look for people whose brands you value for a wide range of reasons. You may value one friend because he cheers you up, another because she's a good listener, or still another because you can count on him to give you a straight answer.

Most people have someone they turn to when they need to relax and laugh, or maybe it's a friend with high energy and an optimistic approach to life whom you can plug into to recharge your own batteries. Those are people with strong Life Brands. They add to the quality of your life. You value your relationship with them. There are undoubtedly other people whom you value for different reasons. Some are life "coaches," who set you straight, urge you to try harder or do more. Others may be spiritual guides, who help you search your soul and find your way. If you are lucky, you also have people in your life who simply love you unconditionally. They love you whether you are up, down, or going sideways.

You may not consciously think about why you buy into the brands of all your friends, but there is something you value about each and every one of them. Have you ever thought about what it is they value about *you*? What do you offer to others in your relationships with them? What does your Life Brand mean to them? Are you a guide, a coach, an energy source, someone they can relax with, or an unconditional love-giver?

Have you ever considered what value it is that you bring to the lives of the people you care about the most? It can be enlightening and maybe a bit scary to ask why anyone should buy into your brand personally. What promise do you deliver on consistently? What do your parents, brothers and sisters, children, and loved ones know about you that they can always rely upon? Is it love and understanding? Is it anger and rejection?

I hope it's the first and not the second, but you should be honest in looking at what it is that you offer in your relationships. If you have had problems building lasting friendships or loving relationships, it is probably because you were getting more than you were giving. You weren't offering anything of real value to the other person. I once knew of a person who had all of the exterior attributes that people find appealing. He was a handsome guy, smart, athletic, and outgoing. Yet, you could see him move from one friendship to the next in rapid order. He would become close friends with someone for a few weeks or months, and then, the next time you'd see him, he'd seem to be attached to someone else. His problem was that he was very self-centered. The guy could not build long-term friendships with other people because his focus was entirely on himself. He formed friendships based solely on what the other person could do for him. If he needed investment advice, he'd befriend someone with knowledge in that arena. If he wanted to improve his golf game, he sought out an expert golfer. There is nothing wrong with building relationships based on shared interests, but long-term friendships are built on mutual respect and mutual interests. If you don't take an interest in the other person's life, you really can't expect that person to want to be involved in yours.

What assets add to the value of your Life Brand in a relationship? Well, what is it that you value in others? What do you look for in forming friendships or loving relationships? Make a list of those assets you value in other people, and then make a list of the assets that you believe you offer them. If you are feeling *real* brave, ask people close to you what they believe you offer as a friend. (Should they need more than five or ten minutes to come up with something, you may want to think about changing your approach to the relationship.)

I believe the strongest relationships are those in which both parties serve each other in many ways. My daughter Wendy brings incredible value to our relationship, and I'd like to think I do the same for her. She gives me energy (though sometimes she does make me feel like an "old guy") while also making me laugh and think. Since she looks up to me as her father, she also makes me want to be a better person. She inspires me to keep expanding my brand so she'll see I am always working to improve myself, which is how I want her to approach life too.

# RELATIONSHIP VALUE EXERCISE

1. What personal traits do you have that add to your value in relationships? (*Examples: A great sense of humor, loyalty, a good listener, concern for others, honesty, generosity, enthusiasm.*)

   _____

   _____

   _____

2. What can you do to build upon those relationship strengths? (*Example: "I'm a good listener but I haven't made the time in the past; I could work on making more time for my children or friends to learn about their lives."*)

   _____

   _____

   _____

3. What do you value in a relationship and how do you reciprocate?

   _____

   _____

   _____

4. What sort of relationships are you looking for? How would you like to change the relationships that you have now?

   _____

   _____

   _____

5. What bad habits do you have that may be affecting the quality of your relationships? What steps can you take to improve?

   _____

   _____

   _____

6. Consider the needs of each person with whom you have a close relationship (your spouse, children, parents, and siblings as well as your closest friends and coworkers). What do they need that you have not been providing? What more can you contribute to your existing relationships?

_____

_____

_____

## YOUR BRAND VALUE IN THE COMMUNITY

In many ways, it is more important to establish a clearly defined brand in this area than any other. People have a greater opportunity to know you personally in the workplace and in your relationships, but more people know you only by your reputation or brand in the greater area of your community. It is easier for people to get the wrong impression of you if they don't interact closely with you. It's also easier to lose control of your image in the community.

Consider what you represent within each of the communities that you belong to. These include any organizations, clubs, or networks you are a member of. If you choose to take an active role in any of them, then you should approach it with the goal of adding value, and not with the attitude of "what's in this for me?"

# COMMUNITY VALUE EXERCISE

1. Think about all of the communities you are involved in. List them, and then for each community you've listed write down any skills, knowledge, or talents that you bring to the table.

   _____
   _____
   _____
   _____

2. What can you do to build upon those strengths in order to add greater value?

   _____
   _____
   _____
   _____

3. Choose one community that you have been particularly active in. Write down the role you play in that community and the things that you've helped accomplish.

   _____
   _____
   _____
   _____

4. List any personal characteristics that you believe you possess that are assets for your communities. _(Suggestions: Leadership, a good teacher, a role model, a calming influence, a catalyst for action, problem solving, etc.)._

   _____
   _____
   _____

5. List any bad habits that may have kept you from contributing more to those communities, and write down ways that you might overcome them.

_____

_____

_____

_____

6. How do you work best in your communities? What can you do in each of them to work more effectively?

_____

_____

_____

_____

## VALUING YOU

The questions you have just answered under each of the three primary sectors of your life—work, relationships, and community—should give you a good handle on your brand assets, the strengths you have and the value you represent in each area. Review the lists you made for each of the three sectors. Are there any talents, skills, areas of knowledge or expertise, and personal traits that appear on more than one list? I'll bet there are. These are your most important assets. They help you to stand out from the crowd. They represent your Life Brand value, and they are the foundation on which you can build lasting career success, long-term friendships, and a legacy in your community.

When you have a Life Brand that offers value to others,

opportunities will come to you. We all look for employees, friends, and community ties that will add value to our own lives. Often, we'll go out of our way to deal with those people, just as we'll pay more for products that offer extraordinary value. For example, I've always had a problem finding shirts that fit me. Most stores don't carry shirts that have long enough sleeves or wide enough shoulders. For a long time, I dealt with this problem by going to tailor shops and having my shirts made for me. Then, a few years ago, a friend, who is a sports agent, told me about Owens & Morgan Custom Tailors and Shirtmakers, which makes custom suits and shirts for several of his athlete clients. This small but thriving company offers outstanding value, and as a result, its brand is growing rapidly in a highly competitive field.

Owner Roy Owens was just nineteen years old when he began working at Leibowitz Menswear, a popular clothing store in his hometown of St. Joseph, Missouri, about forty miles from Kansas City. The owners of Leibowitz, which has been in operation since 1912, prided themselves on making clothes that fit their customers properly. They taught Roy Owens the crafts of measuring, pattern-making, tailoring, and fitting. He worked in his hometown store for five years before taking his skills (brand assets) to a larger employer, the Custom Shop Shirtmakers retail chain, based in Chicago. Roy stayed there three years, refining his craft and learning about the custom tailor business, before he decided to go into business for himself.

"I decided that I didn't want to wake up at age sixty-five and wonder why I had worked for somebody else all my life," he said. "I loved making clothes so I wanted to stay in the business, so I decided to open up my own shop. I moved back to St.

Joseph and started my business, and then I realized I didn't have any customers."

Even before he landed his first customer, Roy decided what the equity or value of his brand would be. "I was a one-man shop trying to compete with huge multimillion-dollar companies," he said. "I decided that I had to perform at a higher level by providing a high level of service and outstanding quality."

Roy knew he would have to supply a lot of value to lure customers away from clothing stores and other custom tailors. He could not undercut the prices of his much bigger competitors, but he could offer more personalized and more convenient service. He took that strength and built upon it. Today, Roy Owens and his sales staff will walk, drive, ride a train, or fly in a plane to reach a customer. They will come to your office, home, gym, country club, or vacation getaway to fit you for suits, pants, and shirts. You can name the time and place.

For busy business executives, athletes, and others who have limited spare time to shop, this personalized service—combined with the custom-fit and fine fabrics offered by Roy's company—is a great value. It must be, because in less than ten years, this small business with only four full-time employees has built a client base of more than 600 customers across the country.

Roy Owens is making a very good living. His company had more than $500,000 in sales in 1999. He is doing what he enjoys doing, and reaping the full benefits of his labors because of the value built into his brand. He looked at his skills as a fitter and merchant tailor and he built his business brand around them. His clothes all carry the Owens & Morgan private label, and now Roy dreams that one day his small but eager-to-please clothing company might be as big as Ralph Lauren's Polo brand.

## WHAT CAN YOU DO TO BUILD GREATER VALUE INTO YOUR LIFE BRAND?

From his custom fitting to his willingness to come to the offices and homes of his customers, Roy Owens has packed value into the Owens & Morgan brand. Like most astute businesspeople, he is always looking for ways to add more value and to widen his customer base. In managing your Life Brand, you should always keep an eye out for ways to build greater and greater value for your target markets.

It doesn't hurt at all to do regular checkups, maybe every three to six months, at least every year, in which you ask yourself, What more can I offer? When was the last time you went to your boss or your biggest client and said that? To your loved ones? To the other members of the clubs, teams, or neighborhoods to which you belong? I'll be suggesting specific ways that you can build value into each aspect of your Life Brand throughout this book, but there are a few general Life Brand assets to consider.

Most of these are simple commonsense things that we all need to be reminded of from time to time. You've probably heard many of these since childhood from the people who care about you. The key phrase in that last sentence is "care about you." Only those who most want to see you be successful and happy will take the time to offer thoughtful guidance. If you practice these assets as part of your daily life, you will never have to worry about "selling" your Life Brand. It will sell itself.

## Life Brand Assets

1. *Listen to others not so that you can respond, but so that you can fully understand THEIR point of view.*

    Have you ever poured out your soul to someone only to have him or her respond with a comment or a story that was completely unrelated to what you just said? You immediately sensed that this person wasn't really listening to you, didn't you? Your trust in that person may have dropped a notch or two because of this inattention. Communication does not begin with speaking. It begins with true listening. It is an art that too many people take for granted.

    Good listening requires serious concentration. It can also be a very rewarding asset. The ability to relate to and communicate with other people may be more of an asset than you've thought in the past. In a study of about 250 entrepreneurs, psychologist Robert Baron of Rensselaer Polytechnic Institute and Gideon D. Markman of the University of Colorado found that people skills are among the traits that produced superior financial performance for entrepreneurs and top executives.

    To be a good listener means knowing when to be silent and when to ask questions that tell the other person that you are interested and involved. It also means that you don't interrupt or try to complete the other person's thoughts. A key point is that even when you may not agree with the other person's point of view, you don't argue or debate; instead, you try to understand the person's perspective without filtering it through your experiences and opinions. Remind yourself that your first goals should not be to convince or entertain—they should be to understand the other person intellectually and emotionally. The emotional aspect is important because often it's not so much what the person is saying that is important, but *how* he or she is saying it.

Listening to understand sounds like a simple concept, but so often we listen only through our own experiences or from our own perspectives. Stephen Covey tells of a father who once complained to him: "I can't understand my kid, he just won't listen to me at all." As Stephen noted, it was the father's failure to listen that was causing the lack of understanding.

The primary reason people don't listen to understand is that it takes a strong sense of self-confidence to allow yourself to be influenced by the opinions and thoughts of others. Often, the natural instinct is to jump in and state your own opinion or to try to influence the person to see your point of view. To provide real value to the other person, you have to be willing to fully understand his or her needs, concerns, and perspective.

Remember, it takes courage to listen without judging. The rewards come in listening to understand. Lyndon Johnson is remembered as one of the most savvy politicians ever to become President of the United States. One of his great skills was listening to others and understanding their perspective. He was a master at building relationships with each representative and senator. As a young senator, he needed a mentor so he went to the top by building a relationship with the Senate leader, Richard Russell. In their conversations, it occurred to Johnson that Russell, who was not married, probably was alone on most Sundays. The young senator began going to Russell's home each Sunday morning to read the paper and discuss politics. As the Pulitzer Prize–winning historian Doris Kearns Goodwin has noted, "Not surprisingly, Russell later helped Johnson become majority leader of the Senate."

2. *Do what you say you will do.*

Again, this seems like such an obvious thing, but there is no quicker way to lose trust and damage your Life Brand than to fail to live up to the expectations you set. On the other hand, there is no greater way to build trust and enhance the value of your Life Brand than to simply deliver on every promise. Mark Twain noted this when he suggested: "Always do right. This will surprise some people and astonish the rest." This applies to every aspect of your life; work, relationships, and community. It relates to the little things that easily become big things, such as not completing tasks on deadline, not showing up, missing bill payments, forgetting meetings, and breaking promises.

Your ability to fulfill those basic tasks is a measure of your ability to fulfill far more complex and demanding obligations. When you do the little things right, your employers and clients, your loved ones, and the people around you are far more inclined to put their trust and faith in you. All Life Brands are built on a foundation of trust and trustworthiness.

3. *Be on time.*

At first, I was going to include this under *Do what you say you will do,* but so many people break this basic rule of etiquette and respect that I want to give it special emphasis. Yes, we are all very busy. Yes, traffic jams can happen. Last-minute things can pop up. There is always another phone call to take. But if you set a time, be there. You can take preventive measures to be sure you are on time by being careful not to overschedule yourself or by building in extra time for potential delays and arrive early if you must, but be there.

This applies to meetings, phone calls, dinner dates, and any other arrangements you set for a specific time. If you are consistently late it brands you as someone who is disorganized, unprofessional, or discourteous. Busy people expect you to respect their time. If you want to establish immediate trust and confidence, show up on time. So few people do it anymore that punctuality alone will help you stand out from the crowd. With everyone trying to squeeze more work into the day, you will be greatly appreciated for making the best of the time allotted to you.

4. *Be a "Good News" carrier wherever you go.*

I have a friend who was known as "Good News" in his office, because every time he came in, he had good news about a sale he'd made, a person he'd met, or simply something he'd heard about. It became more than a nickname for him. It became part of his Life Brand. "It impacted my mind-set and my self-worth. I loved it. My slogan became, 'Underpromise and overdeliver!' " he said.

Too often people misunderstand or misinterpret the idea of adapting a positive attitude about life. It doesn't mean you paste a plastic smile on your face or that you chirp "Have a nice day!" to everyone you encounter. Nor does it mean that you ignore negative things happening to you or around you. It does mean that you realize you always have the choice of how you respond to such things.

Having a positive approach has very little to do with how you appear to other people; it's mostly about how you approach your life. Here's what having a positive attitude should mean to you:

- You try to have a positive impact on everyone and everything within your circles of influence.
- Instead of focusing on problems, you look for solutions.
- Rather than crying or complaining about missed opportunities, you concentrate on preparing for the next opportunities that arise.
- You are happy for the successes of others because you know there is enough out there for everyone.
- You give without expecting something in return.
- You know that what happens *to* you does not change who you are, nor does it mean you cannot rise above it.
- You understand that the choices you make each day determine the quality of your life in the future.
- You don't concern yourself with things that are outside your control. You focus instead on those things that you can influence.

5. *Be determined to work on your dreams every day.*

When I was in my "just drifting along" stage, there weren't any people offering to pick me up and give me a ride to my dreams. But when I began seriously working on myself and my Life Brand, an incredible thing happened. People came out of nowhere to help me. You don't need money, belongings, or a wealth of experience when you set out on your journey to a better life. All you need is a goal and a determination to get it. When you combine those two assets, magical things occur to your Life Brand.

## THE LAND OF LOST-BRAND EQUITY

What happens when a brand loses its value? In the world of product brands, it can be devastating. *Fortune* magazine reported in April of 1999 that one of the clothing industry's great brands was "coming apart at the seams." The company's market share among males ages fourteen to nineteen had been cut in half. It had not had a successful new product in years. Its advertising campaigns had been failures; its manufacturing costs were "bloated." Its biggest customer was quoted as saying that this company was forty-five days late in delivering its products during its most crucial selling season. "Since 1997 the company has announced plans to shut 29 factories in North America and Europe and to eliminate 16,310 jobs. A month ago it said 1998 sales had dropped 13%, to just under $6 billion," *Fortune* reported. The magazine estimated that this great company's market value had shrunk from $14 billion to $8 billion in just three years.

This all happened even though this company has one of the best-known brands in the world: *Levi Strauss*. Can the same thing happen to people who neglect or mismanage their Life Brands? Certainly. How many great athletes end their careers prematurely because they didn't take care of their bodies or because their personal lives were in turmoil? How many actors? How many singers? It happens all the time: A great baseball player ruins his career because of drug abuse. A promising actress takes roles in bad movies and ruins her image. A singer departs from his usual style and loses his audience. It is critically important that you remain focused on your Life Brand and manage it thoughtfully. In the next chapter, I'll show you how to do that.

# Focus Your Life Brand with Success Circles

CHAPTER FIVE

ROSA LOUISE MCCAULEY grew up in Pine Level, Alabama, where she attended the Montgomery Industrial School for Girls. It was a private school devoted to instilling a strong sense of self-worth in the young women who attended. Her mother, a teacher, also taught Rosa to take full advantage of the opportunities that life presented her. History will note that the school and the mother did their jobs well. Rosa Louise's life was not easy, but her moral strength and her integrity became the basis of a legendary Life Brand.

As a girl, Rosa Louise would lie in bed listening to the Ku Klux Klan members ride by on horseback. She once cowered in fear as the racists lynched a black man near her home, fearing they might burn the house down around her, since she too was an African-American. Rosa grew up in a time when blacks were openly persecuted and discriminated against. They could not eat in most restaurants with whites. They couldn't drink out of the same water fountains or live in the same neighborhoods.

Rosa was one of the few black women of her generation to earn a college degree, thanks to her keen mind and strong sense of purpose. While attending Alabama State Teachers College, she married Raymond Parks, and they moved to Montgomery, Alabama. There, they became active in the local chapter of the NAACP, then a young organization devoted to fighting social injustice. By day, Rosa worked as a seamstress at the Montgomery Fair Department Store. She labored in her free time to fight against racial inequality. She tried to bring attention to hate crimes in which African-Americans were flogged, murdered, or raped by whites, yet were unable to get fair treatment under laws that were often written and administered by uncaring whites.

Rosa's goal was to show how racial injustice was bad not just for blacks, but for everyone in the nation. She did not realize, of course, that at the age of forty-two she would come to be seen around the world as a symbol of courage against that injustice.

Late in the afternoon of December 1, 1955, she left work and boarded a city bus to go home. She took a seat one row behind the front section, which was reserved for white passengers. It was the last open seat in the section reserved for black people.

The bus filled up quickly. Soon all of the seats, those for blacks and those for whites, were taken. Still, people kept boarding, and they were forced to stand in the aisles. When the bus driver saw a white man standing, he ordered Rosa and three other blacks seated near her to give up their seats for the white man. Three of them reluctantly got up. Rosa refused. The bus driver threatened to have her arrested. She told him he might just have to do that. The driver stopped the bus and called to a policeman. The driver said he wanted to fill out a warrant against Rosa Parks for violating the town's segregation laws.

## THE POWER OF A LIFE BRAND
## WITH INTEGRITY

Rosa was just one small woman. She had no national platform. She had no political clout. She had no talk show, no radio show, no friends in high places, except perhaps the highest place of all. But she did have a Life Brand that stood for something, so she remained seated until the Montgomery police took her to jail in handcuffs. The arrest of this dignified and respected woman, who had done nothing more than refuse to give up her rightful seat—in the blacks-only section of the bus—highlighted the great injustice of racial discrimination in Montgomery, the South, and across the country.

When word of Rosa's arrest spread through the community, the NAACP leaders called a meeting at the Dexter Avenue Baptist Church, which was led by a new minister in town, the Reverend Martin Luther King, Jr. At the meeting, angry black leaders in the community formed the Montgomery Improvement Association, headed by Reverend King. They also organized a boycott of city buses by African-Americans in protest of the arrest of Rosa Parks and segregation laws. The boycott lasted 381 days, until December 20, 1956, when the U.S. Supreme Court upheld a lower court decision declaring Montgomery's segregated bus seating unconstitutional. It was the first victory in the civil rights movement for African-

Americans and their charismatic leader, the Reverend Martin Luther King, Jr.

Change can be seen as a threat to those insecure about their own place in the world. Racial anger and fear followed the court ruling. Rosa Parks was fired from her job and threatened so often that she and her husband moved to Detroit. It took many more demonstrations and court rulings before most of the nation came to its senses and saw that Rosa Parks had been right all along. Racism hurts everyone.

In the years and decades since the end of American apartheid, Rosa Parks has been honored as a national hero by blacks and whites alike. In the summer of 1996, an audience of nearly 1,000 people, including the President of the United States and members of Congress, rose in their seats to cheer for the petite eighty-three-year-old woman in their midst. Rosa Parks had grown physically frail with age, but her Life Brand was still incredibly strong as she was presented with the Presidential Medal of Freedom, the nation's highest civilian award.

What was it about Mrs. Parks that gave her the power to change a nation? It was the integrity that her Life Brand represented. Like Nelson Mandela, who did not give in to his jailers or betray those who believed in him, Rosa Parks built such a strong brand that she could not be shaken by threats of arrest or violence. She never wavered, and even years after she'd become famous for her courage, she continued to work to bring value to the lives of others by co-founding the Rosa and Raymond Parks Foundation for Self-Development, which has helped hundreds of young people around the country build their own Life Brands of integrity, courage, and strength.

Rosa Parks stayed true to her convictions, and she built a Life Brand that changed history. It's not possible for everyone to have that kind of impact, of course, but her life is an example of the power of integrity to us all. She never let down her guard. She wanted her life to stand for something, and she pursued it with courage and perseverance. "We are here on the Earth to live, grow up, and do what we can to make this world a better place for all to enjoy freedom," she has said.

## BEING TRUE TO YOUR LIFE BRAND

Your ability to build a fulfilling life depends to a great degree on how well you know yourself and how well you stay focused on the things that fire your imagination, creativity, and passion. Rosa Parks never lost sight of her goal. She did not let herself get distracted by fear or anger. She stayed true to her vision, and she maintained the integrity of her Life Brand.

To create a fulfilling and stimulating life you need to build a brand that includes the following:

1. Clear goals that are distinctly defined and offer constant feedback so that you always know where you are in relation to your objective.
2. A focus on your mission so strong that irrelevant events or distractions or worries and concerns are quickly recognized and moved past.
3. The sense that you are in control of your emotions and your responses to anything that happens around you.
4. A driving, natural passion that has nothing to do with money, outside recognition, or power; it's about integrity and self-respect instead.

## THE POWER OF PASSION AND FOCUS

As head of interactive media at Microsoft, Patty Stonesifer built the world's leading consumer CD-ROM business and managed the massive company's investments in online content and services. But she quit when she lost her passion for the job. "My pocketbook, ego and sense of excitement were being satisfied but I no longer had passion for the challenges I faced each day," she told a *Fast Company* interviewer. "Lots of people thought I was crazy to walk away from it all. But I felt like a juggler—managing projects, budgets, and people— whose only mission was not to drop the ball."

She didn't have far to go to find her new passion and a dream job as president and CEO of the Gates Library Foundation, a charity begun by Microsoft chairman Bill Gates. "It aligns my personal expertise and goals with an opportunity to put technology in the hands of people who otherwise wouldn't have access to it," Stonesifer said. "No matter how high your career registers on the conventional charts, you've got to listen to your heart."

Everything you are today and everything that you will be tomorrow are the result of the choices you have made. We make the best choices when we have invested all of our energies, our hearts, and our souls into a course of action that leads to the accomplishment of goals we are passionate about.

We can't effectively pursue goals we don't believe in. You have to follow your instincts and be honest with yourself when asking, "Is this right for me?" That is true whether you are asking about a career choice, a relationship, or a leadership decision in the community.

I spent a good part of my life drifting along because I hadn't developed a passion for anything after my athletic career ended. I'd gone through grade school, high school, and college with a narrow focus; I wanted to play in the NBA. When I wasn't drafted by the pros after college, I went into the U.S. Army for lack of any other plan. While stationed overseas, I landed a contract with a team in the European basketball league so I was able to get a taste of my dream of playing professional basketball. It was a good life and one that I enjoyed for several years. When my playing days in Europe ended, however, I returned to the United States without any solid plan for my future, without a passion to follow, and I now realize, without a Life Brand to build a future upon.

As a result, I drifted into a job with the federal prison system in Denver. I had no particular interest in corrections or criminal justice and so it was mostly just a job, not a career. I did come to see the importance of having a positive impact on such a negative environment and I moved up within the system, eventually transferring to Chicago. I was on a path to perhaps serve as a warden and then move into the executive offices of the U.S. Department of Justice Federal Bureau of Prisons. Still, it was not a career that I had chosen for myself, and I finally came to the point where I asked if this was really what I wanted to do for the rest of my life.

If I had developed a Life Brand at a younger age, I probably wouldn't have found myself in that situation. As a teenager, I'd never planned my life beyond my dream of becoming a professional athlete. After that, I'd just fallen into corrections work. It wasn't until I began meeting and observing people with powerful Life Brands that it finally struck me: I had never clearly defined my vision of success. Oprah is truly a magnet for people who have pursued powerful visions and built their lives around them. I observed the passion that people such as Quincy Jones and Maya Angelou bring to everything they do because they love what they do, and it inspired me to look deeper into my own life.

## A CLEAR UNDERSTANDING OF
## WHAT YOU WANT

To build a truly great Life Brand, you must have a clear understanding of what you want to do with your life, and what you don't want to do with it too. This is one of those rare decisions in life that lies entirely within you. You can't ask your parents, friends, or the career counselor down the street. They all have their own vision of the world and their own perceptions of what you should do with your life based on their experiences and knowledge. This one has to come from your heart. It is so important that you identify your passion and pursue it. If it is a matter of your work life, you should follow Mark Twain's advice by "making your vacation your vocation" and doing what you love. Otherwise, you may get caught up in a job or career that is not connected to your dreams for your life; you face an existence in which all of your energies are pumped out and nothing is pumped in. Stress is the deadly companion of an unhappy heart. It kills people. It kills relationships. It kills dreams.

I've known many stressed-out people who feel they are trapped in dream-killing jobs or dead-end relationships. I also know those who are fully engaged in pursuing their passions. There is no comparison when it comes to the quality of their lives and the power of their Life Brands. One of the marks of a powerful brand of any kind is that it knows itself well enough to select which paths to take and which to turn back from.

Whether it's a brand on the grocery store shelves, a celebrity brand in the world of entertainment, or your own Life Brand, it must be guided by well-defined goals.

## WHEN BRAND INTEGRITY FALTERS, GOALS ARE LOST

Scott Bedbury is widely considered to be responsible for growing the $700 million Starbucks Coffee Company into a global brand with 1,100 outlets serving 4 million customers each week around the world. As senior vice president of brand development, he has put the Starbucks brand on Frappuccino with Pepsi-Cola, and on six flavors of ice cream with Dreyer's Grand Ice Cream, but he once turned down an offer from a company that wanted to create a Starbucks coffee with liquor in it. "We didn't feel it was right for the brand," he told an interviewer. "We didn't do a lot of research. We just reached inside and asked ourselves, 'Does this feel right?' It didn't. It wasn't true to who we are right now."

The brand managers at Starbucks may one day decide that it feels right to add liquor to its products, but the important point of that story is that Bedbury had such a clear vision for his brand that he followed his instincts when it came to keeping it pure and focused. Other major consumer brands have faltered when that vision is lost. Even a real doll of a brand like Barbie.

The all-time best-selling brand-name doll, born in 1959, was experiencing a slowdown in sales in the late 1980s. Her parent company, Mattel Inc., began looking for ways to revive its most profitable brand. A marketing executive, Jill Barad, came up with the idea of creating a higher-profit, limited holiday edition called Happy Holidays Barbie.

This Barbie was priced at more than three times the standard cost for the regular Barbie dolls, which sell for $10. Some executives within Mattel worried that the creation of the special-edition doll might destroy the market for the original, but they were assured that production would be limited to create a demand for the new doll in the collectors' market.

The plan worked beautifully. Holidays Barbie became the hottest doll on the market. That success spawned a whole line of new Barbies from different professions and activities. By the mid-1990s, American girls, on average, had eight Barbies each instead of one. Mattel's Barbie sales rose to $1.7 billion in 1997 from $430 million just ten years earlier.

The marketing executive who had championed the idea of selling Happy Holidays Barbie, Jill Barad, rode its success into the top job as chairman and CEO of Mattel. But then, a critical brand mistake was made. Instead of sticking to the winning philosophy of limiting the production of the special-edition Barbies, Mattel began flooding the market with them in an effort to pump up company profits even more. The company executives who had been concerned about the dilution of the original Barbie brand saw their fears confirmed.

In January of 1998, thousands of Holiday Barbie dolls were still on store shelves after Christmas. The big chain stores began discounting them from $30 to $9.99. "Overproduction of other Barbies and aggressive selling to retailers also were catching up with Mattel," noted *The Wall Street Journal,* which reported that even the most sought after Barbies, which had sold in the collectors' market for as much as $100, were going for $29.99 on the Home Shopping Network.

By the end of 1998, Barbie doll sales were $500 million

short of expectations and Mattel's stock had also dropped dramatically. *The Wall Street Journal* interviewed a disappointed Barbie collector who understood the importance of protecting the purity of a brand. "You don't want to lose an aura," the collector said. "It's hard to win back."

## THE POWER OF KNOWING YOURSELF, YOUR GOALS, AND YOUR PRINCIPLES

Those of us concerned about keeping our Life Brands on track can learn an important lesson from what happened to the Barbie brand when its guardians made poor decisions. The same thing can happen to celebrity brands, of course. Actors have to be careful about which roles they choose and what they do in their lives. One of the most tragic examples of this in recent years is the young actor Robert Downey, Jr., who won an Oscar nomination for his performance as Charlie Chaplin but then lost his freedom to drug abuse. Every attempt was made to help him rehabilitate but, in the end, he was sentenced to three years in prison because he'd lost control of his life to drugs.

There is simply no way that would have happened if the actor had been vigilant about maintaining his Life Brand's integrity. There is great power in maintaining the purity of a brand, whether it is a consumer product brand, a celebrity brand, or a Life Brand. We all have to be vigilant about maintaining the integrity of our brands.

When I first began consciously building mine, I found myself being torn in different directions by people who wanted to buy into my brand for a wide variety of reasons.

They had their own ideas about which directions I should pursue with my brand. Some of them were very convincing. I became uncomfortable, though, because I felt like I was once again losing control. I didn't want that to happen, so I came up with a very basic tool for keeping myself focused on the direction I want my Life Brand to take.

## THE SUCCESS CIRCLES ARE A TOOL FOR CREATING A LIFE THAT FLOWS

Each of us has a certain magic, a gift, a talent, or an ability that if developed and put to its highest use can help us overcome injustices, setbacks, defeats, and difficulties. That magic enables us to use our talents and abilities to make our lives fulfilling and worthwhile and to make the world a better place. University of Chicago psychologist Mihaly Csikszentmihaly writes about "living in the flow." An expert on creativity, he has interviewed hundreds of writers, computer programmers, artists, athletes, physicians, craftsmen, and others about attaining a state of consciousness in which they are so caught up in the pleasure of their work that they lose track of time and most awareness of any outside stimuli. He describes this mental state as "being as close as anything can to what we call happiness." One of the key elements for attaining a life with such "flow" is the ability to screen out distractions and concentrate on your goals and the opportunities you have to pursue them, the psychologist says. Just as a magician needs a wand or a top hat to trigger his magic act, sometimes we need a system for focusing our power to create the magic of flow in our lives.

When I was putting together my goals and a plan to

achieve them for the first time in my life, I devised a system that I call Success Circles. It is a deceptively simple system to help focus your talents and interest as you seek to build and expand your Life Brand. Early in my own efforts to develop a brand, I ran into a very common problem. There were too many paths that looked appealing. I'd make contacts with charitable groups, educators, entrepreneurs, and other businesspeople who wanted to take me in all sorts of directions. I wasn't drifting anymore, but I wasn't going along a path I'd selected either. I was being pulled up down and all around.

Each of us has limited time, energy, and resources. It is simply not possible to do everything, even if some of the options appear to be in alignment with our goals. Deciding which steps to take can be difficult. Effective decision making involves setting priorities and always staying on course to your goals. We can't control time. We can't hold it or put it in storage to be pulled out and used later. But we can decide how we spend it. Wouldn't you rather spend the time you have on your dreams and goals?

The Success Circles are designed to help you live exactly as you want to live and to help you make the most of every minute. Business gurus talk a lot about "time management." Time needs managing only because we never seem to be able to "find" time to accomplish everything we want to do. My advice to you is to stop looking for time. You'll never find it. It's not lost. You're living it. You just have to consciously decide to live it in a more productive way. You have to make time by taking it away from those activities that are less productive than others. You are in control. You should be the one dictating how your time is spent.

One note: In my seminars for individuals, businesses, and organizations, I teach the students to create three circles labeled: *Education, Career,* and *Community* rather than *Career, Relationships,* and *Community.* My seminars are primarily aimed at business groups and organizations, so we don't deal as much in relationships; however, for the purpose of this book about building a brand that encompasses all aspects of your life, I've decided to focus more on relationships. I still believe, however, that an Education Circle, which encompasses all areas of knowledge and expertise, is critically important, because before you can offer value in your relationships, you must build it into your Life Brand.

Let's spend a few minutes now to save you many hours down the road. I want you to evaluate how you are currently spending your time. If you don't like what you find in this exercise you can redirect your efforts and energies. It may take some effort and some self-control, as well as some courage.

## SUCCESS CIRCLES

*Step 1:* Create a list of the activities and commitments that comprise your day. Make your list as comprehensive as possible. List every major category you want to track, everything from eating and sleeping to reading, exercising, driving, and watching television. You may want to be specific in some areas such as "work" so that you can get a handle on exactly what kind of work you are getting done and what you are not getting done. You might want to break it down to show meetings or report writing, telephone calls, commuting, and breaks.

I'd suggest you include virtually every activity in which you are engaged during the average week. The more cate-

gories you create, the more precise and helpful the information.

*Step 2:* Once you've listed all your categories, next write down
your estimate of how much time per week you spend in each.
You can do this in total hours, in percentage of time spent, or
both. Indicate the estimated time for each activity, the ideal
time, and the actual time. Be honest even if it hurts. You may
be tempted to downplay the time spent watching television
and increase the time you spend exercising, for example. To
get the full benefits from this exercise, you must paint a true
picture of your activities during a typical week without vacation days or travel outside the office.

At the conclusion of your week survey, you should have a
realistic accounting of your time. You will have perhaps un-
covered areas where you may be spending too much time and
areas where you aren't spending enough. Based on these findings, you are positioned to make some initial declarations
concerning your future activities. If you did nothing else, this
new level of self-awareness and resolve would be extremely
helpful to you.

Most of those who succeed in achieving their goals do it
by creating an environment for opportunity. They build a Life
Brand on a foundation of knowledge and training and experience. They are always working to expand their influence and
to better their lives by expanding their brands. If you can believe in the possibilities for your life, and if you feel as if you
deserve your dreams and goals, you are well on your way in
this process.

The Success Circles system is designed to help you define, focus, and advance your goals and aspirations. This is a
relatively simple process that when applied thoughtfully and

consistently yields exceptional results. It allows you to build confidence, competence, and capability in all that you do. It inspires you to believe in yourself, in your abilities, and in your power to control your life.

Success Circles teach you to:

o Identify and explore your interests, talents, and skills
o Evaluate and organize your priorities and your time
o Make smart choices and cultivate opportunities
o Foster control and self-sufficiency
o Continuously build value in all that you do

**Step 3:** On a separate sheet of paper draw three circles. These represent your vision, your purpose, your world—the things that define your Life Brand. The goal is to pack your Success Circles with resources that are consistent with your goals and aspirations. This enables you to refine your vision, strengthen your purpose, and create a Quality Life Brand. Label each of the three circles as one of the following:

o My Work
o My Relationships
o My Community

**Step 4:** Consider all of your current roles, duties, responsibilities, and relationships and where they fit within each of these three areas. Each of us has many roles. I'm a father, a son, a brother, a boss, a business partner, a board member, a CEO, and a founder of a charity. I'm also an entrepreneur, a marketing executive, a mentor, a university lecturer, an author, a public speaker, a community activist, and a volunteer for many civic and national organizations.

Write down all of your roles and responsibilities and the activities that go with them. Put each one into the circles in which they fit. Some may fit into more than one circle, which is fine. The objective of this exercise is to get you thinking about the things that give you satisfaction and bring you joy, inspiration, and passion.

*Step 5:* Once you have listed your roles in the proper Success Circles, ask yourself these questions:

o Which roles, responsibilities, and activities do you most enjoy?
o Which are done out of necessity or obligation?
o Are there any that you absolutely dread?
o In which of these do you feel your best?
o In which do you feel least comfortable?

Is there an activity or an environment that you are consistently drawn to? How do you most enjoy spending your time? Do you like to cook? Garden? Work with computers or numbers? Do you prefer music? Art? Sports? Think of the three things that you are the most passionate about. List them in the proper circle or circles.

My own primary areas of interest are marketing, sports, multicultural markets, training and development, and working with young people and public service groups. As you might imagine, there are many activities in each of those categories that fall under more than one of my primary circles covering my work, my relationships, and my community. For example, my role as the founder of Athletes Against Drugs fits into all three categories because promoting the organization is part of my work, many of the people who are involved are long-term friends, and AAD is very much dedicated to community service.

In the same manner, my position as an adjunct professor at Northwestern University's Kellogg Graduate School of Management is an important brand-building part of my career. It also provides a forum for me to give something back to young people by sharing my knowledge and experience in the field of sports marketing while helping foster relationships with young people and the academic community.

In drawing up a chart of my Success Circles, these activities would be located in a portion of the circles that overlap. The overlapping areas represent *synergy*, which occurs when two unrelated actions combine to create more power than either would have produced alone. I've experienced many examples of this in my life but I've definitely become more aware of it since I developed the Success Circles as a way of focusing my Life Brand on the things that matter the most to me.

*Step 6:* When you fill in your Success Circles with the activities that are important to you, life themes should emerge. By examining the contents of the circles closely, you'll be able to identify those things that are most important to you just as I've done. Your next step is to write down what goals you have in each area. If your interests are in music, what is a realistic goal for you? Do you dream of becoming a professional performer or playing in an orchestra, or do you want to become involved in some other aspect such as teaching music, owning a music shop or recording studio, or working for a record company? Once you have identified your long-term goals for each of the Success Circles categories, you can then begin filling in the circles with those activities or opportunities you can pursue to help you achieve those goals.

The Success Circles provide you with a method for strategically managing your life. How? Because they help you eliminate those activities that are not related to your goals and dreams. For example, recently I was approached by a group of men who wanted me to become involved in their plan to build a hotel chain across the country. It was a very nice hotel chain, and they seemed like good businesspeople, but I had only to envision my Success Circles in my mind to determine that it wasn't something I am interested in. The hotel business has nothing to do with marketing, sports, or education, which are the fields that I've devoted my career to. Getting involved in the hotel industry just isn't consistent with my Life Brand, and so I thanked the men and said, "No thanks."

To build a great Life Brand you have to know yourself and understand what you want, what your goals and dreams are. But you also must be able to recognize what is *not* right for you. Often, your instincts will tell you whether or not to take a path that appears on the journey to your goals, but the Success Circles give you a system for making tougher decisions when you might be tempted to wander off the true path. The hotel chain might well have been a good investment of my money, time, and energy. It might have even opened up more opportunities. But I will enjoy much more those opportunities that are in alignment with my own dreams and goals, not someone else's.

## A TOOL FOR CHOOSING WHICH OPPORTUNITIES SUIT YOUR GOALS

"The Success Circles are a tool that help me stay focused," said Paul Bryant, senior vice president for urban affairs at The

Gallup Organization. "As you progress in your career and experience success, your opportunities increase. You get invited to participate in many more ventures, organizations, and social activities. The challenge is to stay focused by recognizing your limitations. You can't do everything, so it is important to concentrate on doing those things that you care the most about."

I met Paul while taking a leadership development course offered by The Gallup Organization, which is based in Lincoln, Nebraska. After he reciprocated by attending one of my seminars, Paul told me that he had been using the concept of Success Circles for a long time without realizing it. Like many successful men and women, Paul had unconsciously worked to build value into his Life Brand over the years. He grew up in Omaha, where he was a standout football player, first in high school and then at the University of Nebraska–Omaha. He was a starting defensive back for three years, and was preparing for the National Football League draft after his senior year when he tore the cartilage in his knee during a touch football game at a picnic.

"The phone stopped ringing almost immediately when word got out about my injury," he recalled. "I was no longer a pro prospect. My dream of playing pro football was gone," he said.

Paul's athletic ability had carried him through life to that point, but his injury dashed his hopes for a pro career. Fortunately, he is one of those people who immediately look for new opportunities when one door closes, rather than focusing on those opportunities that have been lost.

"It was a great lesson in life. It forced me to look for new ways to build value for myself so that I could continue to keep feeling positive about my life," Paul said.

Paul confessed to majoring in "football and girls" at the University of Nebraska. After his career-ending injury, he realized that it was time to hit the books. He looked at his brand assets and realized that while he had great interpersonal and communications skills, he had not taken advantage of the educational opportunities provided by his football scholarship, even though he was the first in his family to go to college. Up to that point, Paul had let life happen to him. After his injury, he took responsibility for the rest of his life by beginning to build value into his brand. When he took that step, he prepared himself for success, and it came.

"As a football player, I got to meet Nebraska alumni who were successful in the business world. They would invite players to their homes for meals and parties. It was the first time I realized that it wasn't only professional athletes who could achieve a higher standard of living. I met architects and consultants and other professionals who had the material things I associated with success at the time. It opened my eyes to the business world. I started taking fifteen to seventeen hours of classes each semester to complete my bachelor's degree and then enrolled in graduate school, where I eventually obtained master's degrees in both urban studies and urban education," he said.

While still in graduate school, Paul realized that he needed real world business experience to go with his growing educational assets, so he offered to serve as an unpaid intern to Bob Armstrong, a dynamic businessman who was the general manager of Enron, an energy conglomerate company in Omaha. "I hung on to that internship for 3.5 years," said Paul. "They did start paying me, but I could have earned more elsewhere. I stayed because I learned so much. Bob introduced me to key players in the corporate community, and showed me how the business world worked."

Paul started a consulting company after graduate school. He worked with the city of Omaha's police department, the YMCA, and the University of Nebraska for nearly four years before joining the First National Bank of Omaha, where he became a bank officer and created a business development department. He left the bank to join The Gallup Organization as national director of marketing, and was promoted to his present position as a senior vice president.

Today, Paul's Success Circles include Urban Affairs, Corporate America, Spiritual Life, Family, and Golf. The golf circle may not be as out of place as it first seems. Paul believes it is important to become skilled at golf because so many corporations and charities use golf outings as networking events. He also thinks his spiritual life and family life (he and his wife have three children) keep him grounded and balanced and enhance his career.

"The circles help me see how these areas of my life are interrelated and they also help me stay focused on those things that are important to my goals. For example, I'd gotten involved with an effort to publish a magazine aimed at women golfers. It matched up with my interests in golf and in business, but after I did a careful analysis of my Success Circles, I realized that most of the work I did on the project involved issues related to printing and publishing rather than those areas that truly interested me. So, I decided it wasn't really serving my goals to remain involved," Paul said.

Think about how this process can work for you. If you aspire to be successful in business, or in athletics or any other field of endeavor, you have to devote yourself to creating and building a Life Brand. You can't let distractions get in your way. The Success Circles help you make those decisions. You can create Success Circles that correspond to virtually every part of your life, although you wouldn't want to have too many going at once. If you use them effectively they will bring consistency to everything you do. There will be synergy between all aspects of your life.

If this process is to be effective, it is absolutely critical that you believe your life can be better. You must feel worthy of success. You must have confidence in the value of your Life Brand. Every person has value. Every person deserves the right to be respected. If you value and respect yourself, your Life Brand will attract people, resources, and opportunities.

# Marketing Your
# Life Brand

CHAPTER SIX

**WHEN CNN ANNOUNCED** in the summer of 1999 that the new anchor team for its widely watched *MoneyLine News Hour* would include a former fashion model with the glitzy name of Willow Bay, *The New York Times* reported that "many in the business world [were led to wonder] if CNN had gone soft."

Up to that point, this beautiful woman with the unusual name had been known primarily as the model for Estée Lauder's worldwide cosmetics advertising campaign. One of her first jobs outside the modeling industry was as the anchor for ABC's *Good Morning America Sunday* entertainment program. She also had cohosted a Saturday-morning basketball show for kids called *NBA Inside Stuff.*

Still, few critics associated this attractive and articulate woman with the serious world of business and financial news. Some rivals in the news business reportedly complained that Willow Bay, a model since the age of fifteen, had been given the prestigious *MoneyLine* job simply because she was young, glamorous, and well connected (her husband, Robert A. Iger, is the chairman of Walt Disney Company's ABC Group), *The New York Times* reported.

What many people did not know was that Willow Bay has a master's degree in business administration from New York University and a serious interest in the world of finance and investing. The problem, then, was not really with her credentials or her ability to do the job; it was in the widespread *misperception* of her as a beautiful woman without a serious side.

To counter that mistaken impression, Willow Bay granted an interview to one of the nation's biggest and most serious newspapers. It was her way of making it known that she was, in fact, more than just a pretty face. "I do not have a wealth of experience in daily financial news reporting," she told the *Times*. "But I do come to this job with a background in business reporting."

Willow Bay succeeded in correcting the limited impression of her talents and ambitions by doing that interview. She also provided a perfect example of someone who refused to allow her brand image to be controlled by outside forces. In doing *The New York Times* interview, she took control of her Life Brand image.

## YOUR LIFE BRAND IMAGE IS THE MESSAGE

Even celebrities have to actively market their Life Brands if they want to keep stretching and reaching for new targets and goals. As a regular person without access to public relations experts, media managers, or press agents, you have to rely largely on what other people think and say about your Life Brand. That's how your market value is determined. If you show others that you are willing to work hard, share your talents, and add value to their lives while enhancing your own, then your Life Brand will flourish. But how do you get the word out about your Life Brand? How do you establish control of your image in your work, your relationships, and your community?

Once you have identified your brand assets and established your goals within the three sectors of your work or career, your relationships, and your community through the use of your Success Circles, the next step is to *market* your brand. You probably have only a vague idea of what marketing is, and little idea of how to apply it to your life. In this chapter and the next, we are going to look at ways for you to establish control of your Life Brand image.

Marketing experts help their client companies determine what consumers want, and then they help the product makers show the target audience how certain features of their products meet their needs. The same process generally can be used to market your Life Brand. You begin by looking at the value you can bring to your work, your relationships, and your community. Next, you analyze the *needs* of your target audience (your boss or your clients, your loved ones, and the people in your community or networks). Then you determine your own *opportunities* for meeting those needs based on your assets (talents, skills, knowledge, and personal traits). After those steps, you devise a *marketing action plan* to communicate your willingness and your ability to meet the needs of your target audience.

Advertising agencies help companies sell products by designing marketing campaigns to make them appealing to you the consumer. When Nike's ad agency wants to market a new brand of Nike rock-climbing shoes, the experts do research to find out what rock climbers want and need from their shoes.

The ad men then design their television, radio, and print ads to show how a pair of Nikes will help climbers meet their needs and achieve the results they desire. The idea is to stress the Nike brand qualities that the people in their target market want.

You have probably gone through this process in the past without thinking of it as *marketing* yourself. But any time you try to positively influence how others perceive you, that is what you are doing. You are marketing yourself when:

o You tell your boss or client that getting the work done on deadline is no problem because you have mastered the job.
o You tell friends that you will "be there" for them whether it involves using your physical strength to help them move furniture, your sense of humor to lighten their moods in sad times, or your mastery of barbecue sauces to give them a good meal.
o You tell a charitable group that you have a knack for planning fund-raising campaigns or that you are willing to volunteer your services on weekends.

## LETTING THE WORLD KNOW THAT YOUR LIFE BRAND HAS SOMETHING TO OFFER

Have you ever wondered why someone with talents and experience similar to yours seems to be more successful, more popular, or more well known in the community? Chances are that you simply have not done as good a job of marketing your Life Brand as that other person. It comes more naturally to some than others, but marketing your talents, skills, knowledge, and positive traits is vital, particularly in the world of work, but also when it comes to relationships and all of the communities you belong to.

Other people are going to form opinions of you whether or not you actively market yourself. They will make judgments based solely on their own perceptions and filtered through *their* experiences and prejudices unless you step in and give them more information. It's up to you to communicate to them if you want to influence their opinions.

It's human nature to form perceptions and opinions of people based on whatever information is available. You probably have pigeonholed people whom you didn't really know based on what they wore or how they carried themselves or spoke. There have been times when you've gotten to know some of those pigeonholed people better and realized how wrong your impressions were; that they had talents and knowledge and personal charms you would have never detected from mere observation. *That's* why it is so important that you actively market your own Life Brand and its public image.

You can't expect others to automatically see all of the value you represent. You have to be proactive in marketing your assets. If you don't control your public image, you will lose control of it just as it happened to me years ago when the media pigeonholed me. I've seen the same thing happen to other people, and I'm sure you have too. Does any of this sound familiar?

*"She's just the boss's wife."*

*"He'll never be able to handle that job; he's just a jock."*

*"Sorry, but you are too young and inexperienced for this job."*

*"We'd like to have you on our committee, but we're looking for someone with better contacts in the community."*

*"Management thinks that after all these years you don't have what it takes anymore to do the work required."*

*"You always seem to be goofing off. Are you serious about any-thing?"*

I can think of great examples to counter the pigeonhol-ing going on in each of those statements. Katharine Graham, for example, spent several decades living under the wide-spread perception that she was "just the wife" of Phil Graham, publisher of the *Washington Post,* the newspaper that her fa-ther had owned. After her husband's tragic suicide, Katharine stepped in as publisher, even though most people in the in-dustry had pigeonholed her as just the publisher's wife. Most thought she was ill-prepared to run one of the nation's lead-ing newspapers.

In her best-selling autobiography, *Personal History,* Mrs. Graham notes that she'd grown up as a pampered but isolated child in a very wealthy family. When she went off to college, she had to be taught how to wash her own clothes. She was the daughter of one domineering and famous man and she'd married another. Even as an adult, she suffered from insecu-rity and felt that most people dismissed her merely as a wealthy man's wife. Yet, Katharine Graham became not only a great publisher but one of the nation's most admired women. She guided the *Washington Post* through the turmoil of the Pentagon Papers, Watergate, and a pressmen's strike, and in the process turned her father's holdings into one of the country's strongest media corporations. Obviously, there was a lot of unknown value in the Life Brand of Katharine Graham all those years. It took a tragedy and many great challenges for her to prove to the world that she was more than "just a wife."

As a former college and professional athlete, I've heard this one myself over the years: *"He'll never be able to handle that job; he's just a jock."* It doesn't bother me because I've known so many great athletes who've also excelled in other areas.

One whom I admire a great deal for both his business success and his quiet leadership is Dave Bing, an NBA Hall of Fame guard who played with the Detroit Pistons. Dave, who was a college All-American while earning a degree in economics at Syracuse University, still works in Detroit, but his team has grown considerably. He is the chairman of The Bing Group, which includes Bing Manufacturing, Superb Manufacturing, Bing Steel, Detroit Automotive Interiors, and Bing Blanking. His companies have annual sales of $225 million and 900 employees.

Dave worked in the steel business for years in the offseason to establish himself before he started his own companies. He understood that he had to market his business talents in order to overcome the perception that he was only a great athlete, but not a great businessman.

## IT'S UP TO YOU TO MARKET YOUR LIFE BRAND

"Garbage in, garbage out" is a commonly used phrase in computer programming that means the computer can only make calculations equal to the quality of information programmed into it. If bad or inadequate information is all that is available, that's all that the computer will generate. The same holds true for people. If you don't give them adequate information about yourself, they'll likely form shallow impressions of you. I've had some problems with this because by nature I'm shy and very private about my feelings. I don't always express myself easily. I've had to work at learning to let people know more about my feelings, my goals, and what it is that I can bring to the table.

One cautionary note: Marketing your Life Brand is *not* about creating a false image of who you are or what you can do. I'm not encouraging you to lie on your résumé, exaggerate about your experience, or claim that you were personally responsible for the creation of the Internet. Marketing your Life Brand is about purposefully developing and making known your talents and characteristics, which can add to the quality of the lives of others.

## THE SELLING OF BRAND-NAME PEOPLE

The concept of marketing people and their attributes as if they were products is not a new one. In the 1950s, advertising wizard Rosser Reeves was hired to help transform a shy military man into a presidential candidate. Reeves used the same techniques he had employed in selling Anacin and other consumer products to repackage General Dwight Eisenhower. He did opinion polls to determine what the American people of that era wanted in a president and then he put the desired words in Eisenhower's mouth in commercials and public speeches. The selling of the president was done with television and radio commercials featuring staged man-on-the-street interviews, clever jingles, and slogans such as "I like Ike."

The Eisenhower campaign was a precursor to similar marketing and image-making programs for other politicians, but the political branding model was itself based on the Hollywood star-making machines that had long been in operation at the major movie studios. As I noted in chapter 3, the big Hollywood studios once created false histories and "star" names for their actors and actresses, but today celebrity branding is much more about aggressive marketing to create greater opportunities. When actors and other celebrities want to market their brands, they tap into an entire industry devoted to pitching and tracking the market value of celebrity brands.

Most celebrities stay in the public's consciousness not because of their wonderful looks or incredible talents but because they follow a professional marketing strategy. They hire public relations experts, press agents, media managers, and others to help them get their names and faces in the spotlight. Their highly paid strategists follow the same step-by-step processes used by the manufacturers of brand-name breath mints, laundry detergents, and carpet-stain removers. They look at the celebrity as a product. They do *market analysis* to see what demographic groups (age groups, men or women, ethnic groups, geographic groups) find the celebrity most appealing and to determine if there are cultural trends that could either threaten or enhance the celebrity's appeal.

A country singer celebrity may change styles or song material if the trend spotters see that music buyers are starting to favor traditional country over country pop. The same applies to celebrity actors. When the action-hero movie genre became hot, we saw a number of actors such as Wesley Snipes, Danny Glover, and Nicolas Cage move away from serious or character roles into high-profile leading roles in action-adventure movies. This was no accident. Their celebrity brand marketing managers did their homework and determined that there were greater opportunities for their stars in that genre.

Celebrity brand marketers also work to build up public awareness of their clients' names. They lobby newspaper and magazine reporters, editors, columnists, and television producers to do stories, interviews, and profiles on their clients to heighten awareness. They also may work to align their clients with major charities, public service organizations, or large corporations to elevate their profiles. That's one reason you see so many celebrities flashing milk moustaches in magazines and from billboards these days.

The goal of most celebrity brand marketing campaigns is to make the individual stand out in the public's memory, to create an image of success, power, and popularity that will enhance the celebrity's earning power and longevity. Successful celebrity brand marketing is the reason that Donald Trump is not just another Manhattan developer, Wolfgang Puck is not just another good cook, and Tiger Woods is not just another good young golfer on the professional tour. Each of those individuals has been able to expand earning power and increase opportunities far beyond those of his or her peers through aggressive celebrity brand marketing.

## MAKING YOU THE STAR

Okay, that's great for all the Donalds, Wolfgangs, and Tigers out there, but what about marketing *your* Life Brand? You can't go out and hire a public relations expert, an agent, and a manager. Chances are if you called *The New York Times* and *People* magazine and suggested they do a story on you, they'd tell you to call your neighborhood newsletter instead. Well, that's a start, and maybe not a bad one.

Remember, your goals for your Life Brand are different from those of Jerry Seinfeld and other brand-name celebrities. Most people with regular jobs outside Hollywood don't find it necessary, or even desirable, to have their names and faces recognized from coast to coast. In other ways, however, the Life Brand goals of most people are more complex than those of the celebrity brand builder. Your Life Brands are more than a career tool. Your objective is a holistic one: to create a reputation for standing out in your work, your relationships, and your community.

You do share *some* of the same goals of celebrity brand makers. Just as every actor who has played the role of James Bond wants to be known as *the* Bond, you want to be known as a star, or a stand out, in your chosen field. The celebrity wants to win the People's Choice Award. You want to be the popular choice in your field of expertise, in your relationships, and in your community. But more important, you want to create a fulfilling and dynamic life.

To do that, you want to be a standout—the person known for setting the standards of excellence in whatever you do. Just as Steven Spielberg wants to be known as the best director, you want to lead your field. Does Spielberg market his Life Brand thoughtfully? You bet! And so should you. "In an increasingly competitive marketplace, [high visibility] is the single factor that explains the difference between a merely competent surgeon and one who earns seven figures and appears on talk shows to plug his or her latest book. It can spell the difference between the modestly successful business consultant and one who's paid $25,000 for a keynote speech," note the authors of *High Visibility: The Making and Marketing of Professionals into Celebrities.*


## TAKING YOUR LIFE BRAND TO MARKET

To market your Life Brand and increase *your* visibility, you can follow the same general strategies as those who market consumer brand products and celebrity brands, with a few adjustments here and there.

### Step 1: Review Your Life Brand Assets

First, let's pump you up by reviewing the assets that your Life Brand represents. Look at the exercises you did earlier on assessing the value of your brand. Go over them again to see if there are any additions or changes you want to make. Review these questions:

o  What special talents, skills, knowledge, and personal traits do you have that might add value to potential employers or clients?
o  What do you offer that might add value to the lives of loved ones and friends?
o  What talents do you have that might add to the quality of life in your greater community, which includes professional associations, service groups, and local, state, and national organizations?

### Step 2: Create a Life Brand Summary Statement

As I noted earlier, other people will form their impressions of you whether they truly know you or not. That is one reason why it is so important to have a clearly defined Life Brand, particularly when it comes to marketing it in the larger arenas of your work and your community, and also in relationships where people often decide whether they want to get to know you better based on your reputation. Wouldn't you rather define who you are than have someone else do it for you?

When consumer product companies market their brands, they begin with very concise statements or summaries of what their products are and where they fit in the marketplace. Seven-Up established its brand as "the Uncola." Avis defined its brand with the slogan "We're No. 2. We try harder." The Volkswagen Passat recently was featured in magazine ads that described it as "The automotive equivalent to the black turtleneck (suitable for any occasion)." Sun Microsystems positioned itself as a power behind the Internet with ads proclaiming "We're the dot in .com."

When consumers see those product ads, they immediately understand where Seven-Up, Avis, the Passat, and Sun Microsystems are positioned in the marketplace. That's what you want to accomplish with a summary statement for your Life Brand. You may naturally resist coming up with a narrow definition of yourself. After all, we like to think that we are multi-faceted and deep-thinking Renaissance men and women with a wide range of interests. For the purposes of marketing your Life Brand to those who don't know you intimately, you have to put your best features forward and then build from there.

Think about all the people you have known through the years. Who stands out most clearly? It was those who had the most clearly defined Life Brands, wasn't it? The bodybuilder in your gym class. The "Brain" in your dormitory. The brownie-making neighbor lady. The funniest kid in your homeroom. The cheerleader. The computer wiz. The all-star jock. Some of them were in control of their images and reputations. Others weren't. They were far more complex than their images, but they made a lasting impression on you because they stood out from the crowd; you had a clear definition of their Life Brands.

Other people you have known made little or no impression. They were like passing scenery because they put out no clear messages about who they were. They simply did not stand out. Is that how you want to go through life? By creating a concise summary statement of your Life Brand, you exert control over your image in your work, your relationships, and the greater community. If you succeed in doing that, you can overcome almost any other prejudicial or negative image that others may attach to your name.

To stand out from the crowd in any endeavor you pursue, you have to offer more value to your target audience than anyone else in your field. If your Life Brand offers great value to your employers or clients, to people you care about, and to your community, you won't have to sell yourself to anyone. They will come to you, and so will opportunities.

Companies that market their brands as "lifestyle products" understand this. Ralph Lauren's Polo ads often feature wholesome, athletic-looking men, women, and children at play in settings so luxurious and inviting that the clothes being worn seem almost secondary. That's because the goal of the ad is to get the reader to believe that purchasing Polo brand products will offer him or her the same elegant lifestyle. "What people feel about themselves is a much greater predictor of buying behavior than who they actually are," said marketing consultant Sam Hill in a *Wall Street Journal* story on lifestyle brand products.

The same principle applies to marketing your Life Brand. Your boss or clients, the people you care about, and those in your community buy into *your* Life Brand because you offer something of value to them. Conversely, if someone feels that there is no value in working with you, having a relationship with you, or inviting you to participate in a communal activity, then he or she won't buy into your Life Brand.

# A VALUE-ADDED BRAND STANDS OUT

In the Midwest entertainment capital of Branson, Missouri, established entertainers such as Andy Williams, Mel Tillis, and Bobby Vinton have their own music theaters, which attract millions of fans every year. But there is another, rather unlikely, performer whose shows attract more tour bus patrons than any other, even though he has never had his own television show or hit record.

This performer is a country fiddler from an entirely different nation. His name is Shoji Tabuchi, and the people who promote tourism in Branson, which has 6.8 million visitors a year, say that he is a "textbook case of word-of-mouth advertising." In other words, he markets his Life Brand with a message that is strong and clear. He offers more value than any other performer in a very crowded and talented field.

Tabuchi was born in Japan and trained as a classical violinist, but in the 1960s he fell in love with country fiddle music while attending a concert in Osaka, Japan, given by country western singer Roy Acuff and the Smoky Mountain Boys. Tabuchi was so taken with the heartfelt power of Acuff's music that he began to teach himself the unfamiliar style by listening to imported country and bluegrass tapes at home.

After getting his college degree, he came to the United States with just $600 and supported himself playing the fiddle in clubs and at fairs. He slowly moved up into nightclubs and then became an opening act for touring performers like Barbara Mandrell and Conway Twitty before landing his first appearance at the Grand Ole Opry in Nashville, where he received a standing ovation and the blessings of his hero, Roy Acuff.

In 1981, Tabuchi joined the growing number of road-weary entertainers who found it easier to settle in Branson and let the crowds come to them rather than touring across the nation. An astute businessman, he opened his own 2,000-seat theater nine years later under the corporate title of Shoji Entertainment Inc.

To overcome skepticism, and perhaps some prejudice, about the concept of an Asian country fiddle player, Tabuchi created a brand image of entertainment excellence and outstanding customer service. His multimillion-dollar light show and music extravaganza, which blends American and Japanese themes, is considered one of the most exciting performances in Branson. But what truly sets him apart from a crowded field of entertainment options in Branson is Tabuchi's devotion to his customers.

Unlike many stars, Tabuchi goes out of his way to meet the members of his audience, even boarding their tour buses to say good-bye after performances. Wheelchair visitors to his theater are provided individual escorts. He also announces birthdays and anniversaries during his two-and-a-half-hour shows, performed two, and sometimes three, times each day from March through December. In addition, Tabuchi provides for the comforts of his guests. He offers fresh orchids and crystal chandeliers in the ladies' rest rooms, where attendants give free samples of Vanilla Waltz hand lotion, a product created by Tabuchi's wife, Dorothy. The men's room has a billiards table, fireplace, and ivy on the walls.

Tabuchi's high level of personal attention to his audience even won over a group of World War II veterans who gather in Branson each year to commemorate a Japanese attack on their aircraft carrier, in which 921 men were killed. When Tabuchi learned that the veterans were seeing his show for the first time, he invited them to his office after the performance. They now return every year.

"Most of the men had mixed feelings . . . But what Shoji has done, he has helped us heal—we're all crazy about him. He came here with nothing and made something of himself," one of the veterans told a *Wall Street Journal* reporter.

Tabuchi became a star and a wealthy man despite some significant handicaps. He did it by creating a clearly defined Life Brand that stood out in a field of stand out performers. What do you think his summary statement is for his career? I'd say it would be something like: *"I will always show gratitude to those who support me in doing what I love."*

What about yours? Do you have a clearly defined image that states your position in the marketplaces of your life? What is the summary statement for your Life Brand? If you don't have it clearly defined in your head, you can't expect your clients, coworkers, friends, or people in your community to have you in full focus. For each of the three sectors, create a one-line summary of what your Life Brand represents. Write them on a separate sheet and keep them for later reference.

Examples:

In my work: *I'm a self-motivated, creative problem-solver.*

In my relationships: *I am trustworthy, dependable, and a great listener.*

In my community: *I am the person to call for help in marketing and publicizing worthy causes.*

### Step 3: Analyze the Needs of Your Target Market
Another obvious key to Tabuchi's success is his thorough understanding of the needs of his target market. Branson is a magnet for senior citizen bus tours and also for families on vacation. He provides wholesome family entertainment in a

plush and accommodating environment. He makes it easy and enjoyable and relaxing for his fans. He knows his audience. Do you know yours? How can you give your bosses, your friends, and the people in your community what they want if you don't understand their needs and how you can best serve them? Political candidates, car companies, and advertising firms spend millions to determine what their target markets want. Isn't it worth your time to spend a few minutes doing the same thing?

First, however, you might want to think about exactly *who* your "customers" are in each of the three sectors we've defined for your Life Brand. Here are a few suggestions:

IN YOUR WORK OR CAREER:
- coworkers
- clients
- supervisors
- customers
- potential employers
- the media covering your field
- awards programs
- headhunters or employment services
- suppliers
- professional organizations
- experts or educators

IN YOUR RELATIONSHIPS:
- spouse
- children
- parents
- siblings
- friends

- coworkers
- grandparents
- other relatives
- neighbors
- mentors and role models
- students
- teachers

IN YOUR COMMUNITY:
- neighborhood groups
- school organizations
- fraternities and sororities
- social clubs
- sporting clubs
- community service groups
- church congregation
- local, state, and national government bodies
- special interest organizations
- hobby groups
- Internet chat groups
- networking organizations
- investment clubs
- merchants

Look at the three sectors of career, relationships, and community and analyze the *needs* of your target market in each sector of your life.

For example:

WORK NEEDS:
- My boss needs fast-working software programmers for a project.

- My coworkers need someone to pitch in during peak periods.
- My customers need customized services.

RELATIONSHIP NEEDS:
- My best friend just lost her father and she is having a difficult time.
- My daughter is worried about getting braces, so she needs to feel attractive and loved.
- My parents need to stay in touch with me to feel like they are still a part of my life.

COMMUNITY NEEDS:
- Elderly neighbors need assistance in carrying and moving things.
- A local boys' club is trying to raise money for a new youth center.
- Our state representative needs more information on our community's industrial development goals.

## Step 4: Evaluate Your Opportunities

Most of us are content to lead relatively quiet lives. We strive to be successful in our careers, to support our loved ones, and to be contributing members of the greater communities to which we belong. We don't want to be celebrities. We just want to be well regarded and respected. We want to stand out but only within our own circles of influence. The way to market your Life Brand in that context is to always be alert to opportunities to contribute. If you are attentive to the needs of others, if you act on your opportunities to be helpful, if you are thoughtful and well prepared, if you keep your promises and remain committed to your ideals and goals, you will never, ever have to *sell* yourself. Other people will do that for you. They will spread the word. That is called *word-of-mouth* or *grassroots marketing* and for most regular people it is the difference between being a stand out and being just another face in the crowd.

It's not what you say about yourself that makes you a stand out, it's what others say about you. Your job is to send out a consistent message that clearly defines who you are. As long as you add value to the lives of people within your areas of influence, they will do your marketing for you. If you want people to recognize the value of your Life Brand, you have to do something to make their lives better. It's as simple as that. If you hope to receive assistance as you work toward your goals, you have to help others achieve theirs.

Evaluate your opportunities to serve the needs of your target market within each of the sectors.

For example:

WORK OPPORTUNITIES:
- My software programming experience and my ability to work under pressure make me a prime candidate for the project at work.
- I could change my work hours to help my coworkers.
- I could find a way to determine the special needs of each customer.

RELATIONSHIP OPPORTUNITIES:
- I recently lost a loved one and I understand what my friend is feeling, so I could be an empathic listener and counselor.
- I could do something to make my daughter feel special.
- I could make it a point to increase communication with my folks.

COMMUNITY OPPORTUNITIES:
- I could be more attentive to my neighbors' needs.
- I could use my contacts to help keep the costs down on the youth center project.
- I could do something to educate our state representative on the needs of people in his district.

### Step 5: Create an Action Plan to Keep Your Promises

You know your assets. You understand the needs of your target market. You see opportunities to serve those needs. Your next step, then, is to communicate your willingness and your ability to take action. To do that, you need a plan.

Examples:

WORK MARKETING ACTION PLAN:
- I will draft a memo noting my experience in rewriting software programs under pressure and my interest in helping on the project. I will then offer to work extra hours and weekends as a team leader.
- I will make arrangements to start coming in early and staying late to help my coworkers get through peak periods.
- I will send out surveys to my customers, and when they are returned I will enter the information into a computer file so that I can provide customized service.

RELATIONSHIP MARKETING ACTION PLAN:
- I will take my best friend to a seminar on dealing with grief, and afterward, I will invite her to dinner once a week until she has learned to deal with her sorrow effectively.

- I will take my daughter out to buy a new dress and then schedule a "date" to make her feel special.
- I will make it a point to call my parents at least twice during the week and once on weekends. And I will plan to spend their birthdays with them.

COMMUNITY MARKETING ACTION PLAN:

- On each Saturday morning, I will check with my elderly neighbors to see if I can help them in any way.
- I will telephone the head of the fund-raising committee and volunteer to serve as a liaison between the boys club building committee and my friends in the construction business.
- I will organize a luncheon for our state representative with our chamber of commerce and local government leaders to bring him up to speed on our industrial development plans.

## Step 6: Sharpening Your Skills

Before you implement your action plan, it's probably a good idea to sharpen whatever skills or assets you plan on putting to use. That may just mean reviewing your research, planning your approach, or contacting the resources in your personal network to make sure the connections are still strong.

Examples:

SHARPENING YOUR WORK SKILLS:

- Before sending the memo, I will read up on the most advanced software solutions applicable for the project, and I will study all documents pertaining to my employer's plan for addressing perceived problems.
- Before I begin working the extra hours, I'll check with

my coworkers to see what additional training I might need to help with the peak demand.

- Before I send the surveys, I'll do a little research into the most effective methods for conducting surveys and getting a high rate of response.

SHARPENING YOUR RELATIONSHIP SKILLS:

- Before I get together with my friend, I'll review books and magazine articles on the best methods for consoling those who are grieving.
- Before I take my daughter out, I'll check the bookstore for books that offer guidance in building self-esteem in young girls.
- Each time before I call or visit my parents, I'm going to sit down and think a bit about all they've meant to me and all they sacrificed so that I adequately convey that I'm not calling out of a sense of duty, but out of love.

SHARPENING YOUR COMMUNITY SKILLS:

- Before I call on my elderly neighbors, I'll check to see if there is any neighborhood news they need to be updated on.
- Before I commit to serving as a liaison for the boys club project, I'll check in with my friends in construction and see what their interests and work loads are, and find out if they know of any others in the building trades who might be interested in volunteering.
- Before I set up the luncheon with the state representative, I'll meet with his top aides to see what sort of information and input he needs to help him in drafting or sponsoring legislation beneficial to the community's efforts.

### *Step 7: Make Your Mark by Fulfilling Your Promises*

Earlier in the book, I explained how a product brand always *promises* something to the consumer. Starbucks offers the promise of high-quality coffee. Amazon.com offers the promise of millions of books ready for delivery to your doorstep. Intel offers the promise of a high-speed processor inside your computer. But what if they don't deliver on the promise? What if your Starbucks coffee tastes like dishwater? What if Amazon.com sends you the wrong book? What if your computer with the Intel inside sticker takes fifteen minutes to boot up your word processor? Well, naturally you lose faith in that brand-name product. And if it repeatedly fails to deliver on the promise of its name, you eventually give up and switch to another, more reliable brand.

The same holds true for the marketing of your Life Brand. It does absolutely no good to analyze the needs of your target markets and to assess your opportunities to serve them if you do not follow through by taking action and fulfilling your promises. Building a Quality Life Brand can take a lifetime. It takes patience and perseverance and commitment. The top brand in baby food, Gerber, shows its commitment to its target market by offering a twenty-four-hour, toll-free, no-strings-attached hotline for parents with questions about their children's food. How can you show your commitment to your target markets? By fulfilling your promise to always add value to their lives while building value in your Life Brand.

It's not easy building a Quality Life Brand. Believe me. I struggled for many years in trying to take control of my brand. You can't let minor setbacks get you down. I've found that often, just when you think you've hit the wall, you experience a breakthrough that takes you to new heights of accomplishment. I've experienced it, and I've seen others do it too.

A few years ago, Jesse Brown became a stockbroker in the Chicago office of one of the major investment firms. As the new guy and the only African-American in his office, Jesse had a hard time at first. He'd make "cold calls" to try to win clients but it was tough to win the trust of strangers. He watched in envy as some of the more experienced brokers in his office seemed to effortlessly earn big commissions by chatting with their clients and getting referrals for new business from them. After several months, Jesse asked one of the top brokers in his office how he'd built up his client base. The successful broker told him that he had identified a niche market and focused on it "until I owned it."

The broker had found his niche in an unlikely place. He had long been a fan of classical music by Johann Sebastian Bach. In fact, he was president of an organization for people who shared his musical tastes. He offered his services as a broker to people in the organization and soon he was widely known as the stockbroker for classical music lovers around Chicago and beyond.

When Jesse thought about his coworker's success with his niche market, it occurred to him that as the only African-American broker in his office—and one of very few in the entire industry at that time—he could probably carve out a sizable niche by marketing his services to the growing numbers of blacks seeking to build wealth in the stock market in order to purchase homes, finance college educations, and prepare for retirement.

Jesse did not have to hire a press agent or a publicist. He simply began to market himself by talking about the value of building a thoughtful long-term investment strategy to other African-Americans in his church congregation, in his Masonic lodge, and in his fraternity's alumni group. Not surprisingly, he found a very receptive audience because few other stock-brokers had realized the enormous potential of the African-American market. Jesse worked hard to "own" that market by speaking to other black congregations and organizations. He also became a big advocate of black investment clubs and a popular speaker at their meetings.

Jesse Brown became a standout in his field and also in the black community because he encouraged African-Americans to follow wise investment practices and build wealth. As a result, when the media went looking for sources on the growing number of African-American investors, they found Jesse Brown. *The Wall Street Journal* did a profile of Jesse and his work with black investors, which led to his being offered a book contract worth several hundred thousand dollars. His book, *Invest in the Dream,* made him a nationally known authority on African-American investing and opened up a wide range of new opportunities for him.

Jesse Brown never dreamed that his efforts to find a niche market would bring so many rewards. After all, he started his campaign humbly, in his own church and social organizations. You can't get any more grassroots than that, and yet he is now recognized around the country as an authority in his field. The same thing happened to me, and it can happen to you too.

# Expand Your Brand!

## CHAPTER SEVEN

**TEN YEARS AGO,** Faye Childs was a frustrated writer. She had written a book she was proud of, but she couldn't get a literary agent to represent her. Thousands of aspiring writers face the same situation. It's almost impossible to sell a book to a publisher without a literary agent, and most reputable agents receive so many unsolicited manuscripts that they rarely get to go through them all. As an African-American woman, Faye felt that her road to literary success was even more difficult because at that time there were not many black authors represented in the market.

Some writers just keep writing without ever having any hope of being published. Some settle for publishing their own works, or submitting them to small presses or literary journals for publication even though the audiences are relatively small. Others just give up altogether.

There isn't any "give up" in Faye Childs. When the single mother of four from Columbus, Ohio, ran into roadblocks in her efforts to get her book published, she simply took a new route. She believed that at the root of her problems was bias in the publishing world, which, like most businesses, is primarily run by white executives. Faye saw that people in the publishing world simply were not aware that many African-Americans were avid readers, but that there weren't many published books written from their perspective. She decided to do something about that.

"I was angry with the widespread misperception in publishing at that time that black people didn't read and didn't buy books and that there was no African-American market for authors. That was the overall perception as late as 1990, and I wanted to find out what it was based on. I am an African-American woman and I'm an avid reader. So are most of the black women I know," she said.

Part of the problem was that for many years there were very few blacks working in positions of power within the publishing industry. Faye found that there were so few prominent black authors that publishers concluded, out of ignorance or racism, that blacks didn't read, write, or buy books. In her research, she also noted that very few African-American authors made the prestigious *New York Times* best-seller list.

"I decided that if that was how the publishing industry was going to define success, then I was going to help change their definition and their perception of the African-American market," Faye said.

In 1991, Faye and her sister, Noreen Palmer, launched the BlackBoard African-American Bestsellers List. Their goal was to celebrate black writers and those books written from their perspective, and to promote literacy in the African-American community. The sisters compiled their list by polling independent bookstores around the country. They then convinced the *New York Times* syndicate and the publisher of *Essence* magazine to publish the Blackboard Bestseller List on a regular basis.

The publishing world took notice. The American Booksellers Association invited Faye and Noreen to host a reception for African-American writers, publishers, and booksellers—as well as anyone else who wished to attend—at its annual convention, which draws the leading writers, agents, editors, and publishers from around the world.

Soon, the sisters from Columbus found themselves hosting and getting to know literary luminaries and celebrities such as Maya Angelou, Terry McMillan, Bebe Moore Campbell, Iyanla Vanzant, Walter Mosley, Tony Brown, Nelson George, South African Archbishop Desmond Tutu, Suzanne Taylor, and many others.

The BlackBoard List of African-American Bestsellers had more impact on the publishing world than Faye and Noreen dreamed possible. Their campaign to highlight the works of black authors caught the media's attention. More than 300 national newspapers and magazines wrote about BlackBoard. Many of the articles noted a "trend" in which African-Americans were eagerly buying books that dealt with issues from their point of view. Publishers and agents jumped on those reports and began actively seeking African-American authors and their works.

The sisters did not make any money from their Black-Board Bestsellers List. That really wasn't their goal. They had just come to feel passionate about the publishing world's failure to recognize black authors and the African-American market. They accomplished their mission and helped many black writers reach an audience for the first time. In addition, Faye and Noreen created the Blackboard Literacy Initiative, which brings touring book authors into city and private schools and service organizations in the black community. "We've been told by teachers that the kids in their schools would never have had the opportunity otherwise to meet black authors who can serve as role models and inspire them to read and learn more," said Faye.

In the process of doing all of this for their community, Faye and Noreen earned the recognition and respect of authors, agents, publishers, booksellers, and readers. "We've been branded. We now have widespread name recognition. Many books in the stores currently carry a sticker saying 'Blackboard Bestseller!' and that has given added prestige to the authors while also marketing our list," said Faye.

Without thinking about it, the sisters built added value into their Life Brands too. They have benefited in many ways, but one of their greatest rewards was the acceptance of their nonfiction manuscript by an agent and a publisher. Their book, *Going Off,* is a guide for African-American women on how to effectively deal with anger. The sisters offer a great example of two women who got mad, and then got ahead by doing something that improved the lives of everyone in their community. Faye and Noreen created BlackBoard for the benefit of all African-Americans, readers and writers, and, as so often occurs, they reaped many benefits themselves.

I've seen it happen many, many times. While some may think they have to fight their way to success, perhaps hurting others along the way, I've seen so many people lead happy and fulfilling lives of real achievement by focusing instead on helping others. It has happened to me too.

## TRUE SUCCESS LIES IN
## HELPING OTHERS SUCCEED

Back in 1985, I was still working at the Metropolitan Correctional Center federal prison in Chicago. I wasn't a well-known public figure. I wasn't on anyone's A-list, B-list, or C-list. I was just a regular guy in a regular job taking home a regular paycheck.

But I got involved in a project that turned out to be one of the greatest things I've ever done to market my Life Brand—even though I wasn't thinking about my brand or anybody else's when I did it. It just happened because I believed something had to be done.

I was no longer a professional basketball player at that point, but I still considered myself an athlete, and I'd grown weary of the bad press and media outcry about drug use by certain high-profile sports figures. From all the media attention, you might have concluded that everyone involved in sports of any kind—basketball, baseball, football, track, tennis, hockey, golf, and badminton—was a drug user or an alcoholic. I knew that was not true. Athletes cannot consistently perform at high levels if they are putting toxic substances in their bodies. Most professionals are very careful even about what they eat because they know their careers and their livelihoods depend on being in top physical condition.

I found it disturbing that the public image of athletes everywhere was being damaged because a small number of people had admitted to drug abuse. Mostly, I was concerned that young people who often see athletes as role models would get the idea that to be good in sports you *had* to use drugs, or that it was cool to get high. I worked in the prison system. I saw where people who abused drugs and alcohol ended up. It wasn't in the winner's circle.

Many of my friends in Chicago were athletes, and when I talked to them they were equally concerned. I'd met Michael Jordan a few years earlier when a friend asked me to be his stand-in during production for a commercial he was doing. We were the same height and build, and I did it just for the fun of it. After that, whenever Michael was doing another commercial, they'd call me to help. The Bulls weren't winning much back in those early days, so he wasn't quite the huge celebrity that he eventually became. We got to know each other and we saw each other socially from time to time. I asked him and a few other professional athletes I'd come to know—including Gale Sayers, Otis Wilson, Sid Luckman, and a few other Chicago Bears veterans—if they'd support me in establishing an organization devoted to telling young people that drugs are dangerous and unhealthy. They all agreed to lend their names to my project.

I started Athletes Against Drugs with nothing more than an idea and the support of those friends in the athletic community. Chicago lawyer Mitchell Ware agreed to be the chairman of my board of directors, and he let me use an office in his law firm as the AAD headquarters for a few years.

Today AAD's membership includes more than 150 drug-free athletes. Among them are Michael Jordan, Evander Holyfield, Tiger Woods, David Robinson, Isiah Thomas, and many others. Our programs to teach drug awareness and leadership have reached more than 12,000 elementary and high school students, and just recently, we began a College P.R.E.P. Program to help deserving high school student-athletes develop into leaders and scholars.

While I was working to create, develop, and build Athletes Against Drugs into a national nonprofit organization I wasn't thinking at all about what it might do for *me*. I had a passion for athletics and I wanted to do some good work for my community and for young people around the country because I was concerned. But I learned a lesson along the way. I learned that one of the best and most rewarding ways to market and expand your Life Brand is not to seek public recognition, but to earn it.

## EXPAND YOUR BRAND AND
## NEVER STOP GROWING

Let's look at the concept of "expanding your brand." When I use that term, I'm referring, primarily, to widening your success circles by reaching out to new markets where you can put your gifts to even greater use. We all come into this world with a very limited reach. As infants, our circles are pretty much confined to our parents, whom we influence by smiling, sleeping, crying, and doing the other things that babies do. Our circle expands quickly as we grow older. It begins to include our extended families, friends, neighbors, teachers, classmates, and others. Our ability to influence them also increases as our communication skills broaden to include conversation, writing, public speaking, book writing, filmmaking, and so on.

At some point, our circles usually stop growing. We find ourselves living a limited life, going to work, coming home, seeing the same people socially, and generally staying within a comfort zone. It's a plateau that we will never get off unless we consciously work to expand our success circles in each sector of our lives. There is nothing wrong with being comfortable with your life, as long as you are truly happy and fulfilled. If you've done all you want to do in life, shared your gifts to their fullest, then you probably have no desire, hidden or otherwise, to expand your Life Brand.

If there is still more you hope to accomplish, new markets you want to reach, a wider circle of friends you want to create, or if you want to have an even greater impact on the world around you, then the way to do it is to expand your brand. It's up to you. You can't sit around and wait to be discovered. They don't give "genius grants" to people just sitting on the porch in a rocking chair. The odds are pretty strong that Ed McMahon and Dick Clark aren't going to come knocking on our doors with a check the size of the dining room table. If you want more out of life or if you sense that you are growing stagnant, you have to reach beyond your self-imposed barriers and limitations. You can do that by expanding your brand.

Esther Dyson was working on Wall Street in the early 1980s when she decided that she was losing interest in her work. She took a big pay cut to leap into the world of the Internet, where she is now regarded as one of the most influential commentators on its impact and its future. "The world around you keeps changing and if you can't change with it, you're in trouble. So develop ways to open your mind," said Dyson, president of EDventure Holdings, in a *Fast Company* interview. "Don't always read the same section of the newspaper first. Don't always visit the same Web sites. Look for adventure. If you feel as if you can't get better at something, do something else."

## REACH OUT WITH YOUR GIFTS

You can expand your brand by finding new ways to reach out to your target markets in your work, your relationships, and your community. It's simply a matter of identifying new ways to add value by offering your talents, skills, and knowledge. You do not do it by trying to be all things to all people.

As Dyson noted, you don't have to stick to one job. In most cases, your talents can be put to a wide range of uses, and sometimes you may find more rewarding outlets. A writer, for example, may find security, but meager financial or personal rewards, working as an advertising copywriter. There can be more substantial monetary rewards and creative pleasure in writing for big-city newspapers, national magazines, and book publishers. It's important to stay focused and within your Success Circles so that your brand image remains clear. The same principle holds true in the branding of consumer products.

When brand names are spread too thin, the target audience often gets confused and loses interest, even in brands that once inspired loyalty. Do you remember your first credit card? Mine was an American Express card. In the 1980s, it was considered prestigious to have an American Express card. Remember their slogan, "Membership has its privileges"? It was the dominant credit card in the market. But as competition from other credit card companies increased, American Express diluted its brand image of exclusivity and prestige by issuing a wide range of cards, including specialized versions for students, senior citizens, and corporate employees—not to mention the gold and platinum cards as well as the whole family of Optima cards.

Instead of making American Express stronger, the new versions diluted its brand image and its appeal. The company lost market share to its competitors. By issuing dozens of new cards each year, American Express tried to be everything to everybody. You should not make the same mistake with your Life Brand. Think again about what *Forbes* magazine said about Jerry Seinfeld. He was described as a "pure brand" because of his decision to stick with comedy as his focus and to build his brand from that framework. He has earned millions and millions by keeping his focus narrow but far-reaching.

## USE YOUR SUCCESS CIRCLES TO STAY FOCUSED WHILE STRETCHING OUT

Your Success Circles can be particularly helpful in keeping you from diluting your own Life Brand. Your goal should be to expand your circle of influence within your narrow focus of interest as defined by your Success Circles. If your interest is in music, you can expand your Life Brand within the field of music by performing, composing, working as a critic, leading an orchestra, mastering new instruments, recording, or promoting the works of other artists. But you wouldn't want to expand your brand by stepping outside your circle to get a medical degree, would you? That would take you totally out of your field of expertise and your Life Brand would diminish.

You can see the effectiveness of this *narrow but far-reaching* approach to branding in consumer products by taking a look at Subway, the fast-food chain begun in 1965 by Fred DeLuca. He was just seventeen years old, fresh out of high school in Bridgeport, Connecticut, and looking for ways to save more money for college. His job in a hardware store wasn't paying enough. One of his parents' friends noted that there was a sub sandwich place in his hometown that seemed to do a lot of business. Since this friend was a bit of a brain, a nuclear physicist, DeLuca took his suggestion seriously—and then he asked him for a $1,000 loan so he could open his own store. His first location, near the hardware store, wasn't a very good one, which made DeLuca realize that it was important to stand out, so he used a bright yellow logo and opened his next two stores in better locations.

From the start, DeLuca felt the way to build his business was to focus on one thing—good subs—and to stand out from the crowd by having high brand visibility. He decided to do that by having *a lot* of stores. Within thirteen years, he had 100 locations, most of them franchises. By the late 1990s, Subway had 13,840 restaurants in seventy countries, and both DeLuca and his early backer were multimillionaires and co-owners of one of the most successful and *highly visible* food franchises in the world.

## REACH OUT AND EXPAND YOUR BRAND

So what can you learn from a ham, cheese, salami, and tomato sandwich shop? The fine art of expanding your brand. Fred DeLuca's strategy of staying focused with his menu but maintaining a high profile with his stores has paid off. The same strategy can work for you too. By getting involved in a variety of activities and organizations that reflect your particular interests and passions, you can showcase your brand assets— your talents, skills, and knowledge—while making a contribution. Creating Athletes Against Drugs turned out to be the first step in my own Life Brand expansion process. It gave me much more visibility and increased my success circles tremendously.

As Athletes Against Drugs—AAD—became recognized in Chicago and around the country, I suddenly found myself in the spotlight as a spokesman for the antidrug movement in athletics. When newspaper, magazine, and television reporters looked for balance on the issue of drug and alcohol abuse by athletes, they came to me as the spokesperson for AAD.

The notoriety was something I had not considered when I founded the organization, but it proved to be very helpful when I left my job with the federal bureau of prisons and began my career in public relations and marketing. When I met people, I wasn't just a guy trying to make it in a new field, I stood out as the founder of a community service, nonprofit organization, which I'd taken from the grassroots into a nationally known entity. Suddenly I had a Life Brand that was very marketable, and it was mostly because other people recognized my efforts. I didn't have to *sell* myself by hiring public relations people or press agents; my Life Brand grew because others felt I had earned it.

In the years that followed, I found many other opportunities to extend my reach while staying focused on the things that most interested me. A great opportunity came along when I was asked to write a regular column on sports and sports marketing for *Inside Sports* magazine, which helped position me as an authority in the field and increased my visibility. I also stretched my professional brand by teaching sports marketing, first at George Washington University's Forum for Sport and Event Management and Marketing, where I was the founder and first director. Currently, I teach both a sports marketing and a leadership course at Northwestern University's Kellogg Graduate School of Management.

I've done a great deal of stretching and reaching out. I've worked hard to expand my circle of friends and to bring more value to the lives of people I love. I've done the same in my communities, even in the town where I grew up, Whitesboro, New Jersey, where I founded Concerned Citizens, a grassroots service organization to get residents involved in making the town a better place to live and raise a family. All of these activities, along with my involvement with many national and local nonprofit and service organizations, have increased my visibility and subtly but effectively helped me market my Life Brand. The rewards have come in many different ways, but mostly they have made the quality of my life richer and more meaningful.

## EXPAND YOUR BRAND BY BETTERING THE LIVES YOU TOUCH

There are many magazine articles, and even a few books now, that urge people to package and sell themselves like products in the workplace and job markets. The idea of *selling* yourself doesn't appeal to me. It conjures up images of a hustler, someone who uses glad-handing, back-slapping, and insincere behavior to ingratiate himself. When I sense that people are working too hard to "sell" me on themselves or their services, it makes me uncomfortable. Like most individuals, I'm much more likely to be impressed with someone who has come to my attention because others are enthusiastic about that person.

I didn't understand the distinction earlier in life, particularly in high school. Most teens don't. In their immaturity, they think that they have to stand up and shout to be recognized. They don't realize there are much better ways to stand out, and that recognition comes when you make a real contribution. I was a good basketball player in high school but I wasn't secure enough to let my actions on the court speak for themselves. I was boastful. I felt I had to tell people about my accomplishments in order to build my reputation. When I was named to the All-State team, I wanted the principal to announce it on the school's public address system. I just wasn't secure enough to trust that people would find out on their own eventually. I didn't realize then that what others say about you is far more powerful than what you say about yourself. I wanted the recognition right away. I felt I had to promote myself. I was wrong. I should have worked instead on *improving* myself by investing my time and efforts to better the lives of people around me.

Self-promoters stand out because they do all they can to get ahead. But often they stand alone. It's those who give of themselves who attract a lasting crowd of supporters. It's one thing to consciously accept responsibility for marketing your Life Brand. It's another thing to be manipulative and insincere in order to push yourself ahead. So what are your choices? Is there a way to stand out from the crowd without being manipulative or a self-promoter? Or is the answer to do nothing and just hope that good things will come your way?

We all like to think that our talents and personal charms will naturally attract job offers, promotions, friends, and public recognition. Unfortunately, it doesn't always happen. Look around your office or community and I'm sure you'll observe that many of the most talented, knowledgeable, and good-hearted people are passed over while others with perhaps less going for them somehow manage to move up the ladder, win awards, and move into leadership roles.

It's not that these achievers are more (or less) deserving of recognition and success. It's just that somewhere along the line, they realized the importance of creating, controlling, marketing, and always expanding their Life Brands. The secret is to do it in a manner that builds a lifetime of continuous achievement and fulfillment. That means you don't promote yourself by bragging, exaggerating your accomplishments, or demeaning or climbing over others. It means you don't build your Life Brand on a shaky foundation. You build it on the rock-solid principles of honesty, integrity, trustworthiness, and concern for the welfare of others.

The most effective way to expand your Life Brand, then, is not to be manipulative, or phony, or to engage in blatant self-promotion. *It is far better, and more effective over the long term, to stand out as someone who builds value in his or her own life by consciously and consistently working to add value to the lives of others.* Does this mean your role model should be Mother Teresa? Not necessarily. Does it mean you should ask for a raise for your coworkers instead of asking for one yourself? No. It simply means that when your focus is on giving instead of receiving, a certain chemistry occurs.

How does it work in real life? I've told you how it worked for me after I began Athletes Against Drugs, but you may feel that I had some distinct advantages. I admit that not everyone can get Michael Jordan on the phone to help launch a project. So, let me tell you about Marjorie Landale, who quietly has made a difference in her work, her relationships, and her community.

## STANDING OUT BY REACHING OUT

Marjorie—or "Margie," as she is known—is a night manager at the Regent Square Tavern, one of three neighborhood establishments on a single block in Swissvale, a community near Pittsburgh's East End. Although she is not a celebrity, or a powerful person with money and status, Marjorie was featured in *The Wall Street Journal* as "proof of the difference one energetic employee can make." I read the article about her, and it struck me as a great example of the wonderful things that can happen when you focus on bringing value to the lives of others; so we interviewed Margie to get the story straight from her for this book.

When the Regent Square first opened in 1991, Margie became friends with a customer named Lenny Visco, a building contractor with eleven brothers and sisters. Lenny also happens to be deaf, as are six of his brothers. Another family member has very limited hearing. The Viscos lived near the Regent Square's neighborhood, but many other hearing-impaired people also frequent the establishment because it is just a few blocks from a satellite branch of the Western Pennsylvania School for the Deaf.

The Viscos and their friends use sign language to communicate with each other. Margie caught on to the hand signs they used to order food and drinks, but they often teased her that if she was seriously interested in her customers, she should learn to communicate in their language. "After a while, I decided it probably was more reasonable for me to learn the basics of their language than for them to start using mine," Margie said.

She did just that. She enrolled in sign language classes at the Center for Deafness, paying the $50 fee herself. "I really didn't do anything special. I just took a couple courses off and on over a few years. I did it to make the people coming in more comfortable so when they walk in they always know there will be someone here they can communicate with easily, without having to write things out on a pad," she said.

While Margie is modest about the effort she made and a little embarrassed at all the attention she's gotten for it, she did make an impact. While learning sign language, she befriended faculty members at the Center for Deafness, and soon they started coming into the Regent Square, along with more of their students. To further accommodate their growing clientele, the Regent Square's owners put in a special text-transmission phone system and a captioned television.

Now there are nights when 90 percent of the customers at the Regent Square are hearing-impaired or sign language instructors. "It's not just because of me," Margie insists. "We do have a nice place here too."

## BENEFITING OTHERS AND
## REAPING THE REWARDS

I'm sure Margie did not enroll in those sign language classes with lofty thoughts of enhancing the value of her Life Brand. She probably wasn't even thinking about helping bring more customers into the Regent Square. She simply wanted to be able to communicate better with her customers and friends. But in taking the classes and learning sign language, she changed her life and the lives of those around her. She became a standout not because she demanded attention but because other people appreciated what she did. By taking the time and making the effort to master a new skill, Margie:

1. *Made herself all but indispensable to her employers at the Regent Square.* As a modest person, she denies this, but her communication skills have brought in more customers and attracted national media attention.

2. *Greatly widened her circle of friends and her circle of influence.* "Lenny now has me introduce him to potential customers, and I help them understand sign language. He's asked me to wear a Visco Construction T-shirt and to pass out his business cards but I've drawn the line at that," she said with a laugh.

3. *Made a significant contribution to her neighborhood and her community.* "I have been able to talk other people—including some of my nieces and nephews—into taking sign language classes by explaining how much easier it is than most people think. Several have thanked me because they've enjoyed it so much," she said. "They understand now how we tend to classify deaf people as a group but when you learn sign language you can communicate and see them as the individuals they are. I know that before I learned to sign, I had always thought of one customer as a very angry guy because of the way he signed, but I learned that it's his mannerisms," she said. "Most of the problems deaf people have aren't caused by their hearing problems; they are caused by people with preconceived notions about them. I understand that now."

4. *Enhanced the quality of her own life and the lives of those around her.* "You know, it's amazing to me to realize that there is this whole other culture within our society that so many of

us know nothing about," she said. "The deaf culture is very different from what most of us have experienced. Even if you can sign and communicate, you don't understand it fully. One of my friends said he has taught sign language and interpreted for the deaf for many years but every time he thinks he has come to understand their culture something happens that makes him aware that he still has a lot to learn. I know I've learned to be more patient not just with my deaf customers but with people from other cultures too. It's just taught me to be more understanding."

I think we can all learn from Margie's example. She is a regular person who became a standout in all areas of her life by increasing the value of her Life Brand. Her story is proof that you don't have to be a celebrity, a millionaire, or a supremely talented person to stand out from the crowd. You don't have to build a billion-dollar company, rescue children from a burning building, or hit seventy home runs in a single season to be considered someone special. You can distinguish yourself by thinking about the needs of others and then taking whatever opportunity you have to address those needs. Margie's efforts to learn sign language demonstrated that she is a caring and concerned individual willing to go the extra mile. Because she made the effort, she has become a celebrity of sorts. She's the person sitting in the crowded theater while everyone else stands and applauds her. And that's a great place to be.

In some cultures around the world, it is considered unacceptable to try to stand out from the crowd or to call attention to yourself. Fortunately, we don't live in such a place. We live in a country that encourages individuality and initiative. You can see this in every aspect of our culture. In art, sports, literature, and in business too, the people who most often succeed are those who stand out from the crowd by building lasting value into everything they do. They appreciate and honor the talents, skills, and intelligence that they've been blessed with. And they appreciate those same things in others.

What can you do to offer value to others while displaying your Life Brand assets? I've put together a list of suggestions to get you started. Keep in mind that your goal with each of these is to first offer something of value to others. You shouldn't expect or demand to receive anything in return.

## NINETEEN WAYS TO EXPAND YOUR BRAND

1. *Start a nonprofit service or charitable organization.*

    Does your community have a Big Brother/Big Sister program? A Junior Achievement chapter? How about a literacy program for underprivileged children? Or a Meals on Wheels program for the elderly? Every community has special needs, and if you have an interest in serving others there are certainly many outlets for your particular talents, skills, or knowledge. Founding a chapter of a service organization is a great way to add value and subtly market your Life Brand.

2. *Create a newsletter or Internet e-zine for your business, profession, hobby, or neighborhood.*

    If you are skilled in writing or the graphic arts, publishing a newsletter in print or on the Internet can be a good way to add value and showcase your assets. Maybe the company you work for or a professional organization you belong to is in need of a monthly newsletter, or perhaps it's your child's school or athletic organization. Newsletters are widely read and, if they provide useful information, greatly appreciated.

3. *Write articles for publications in your business or community.*

   If there are already newsletters and bulletins being published by your company, professional organization, neighborhood group, or church congregation, you might consider writing articles or offering to do a column for them to establish yourself as knowledgeable and as an active voice.

4. *Start a professional organization.*

   It takes initiative to form an organization to serve a need within your profession, and executives and managers rarely fail to notice when someone is willing to take on a leadership role. If you sense a need within your profession for any sort of group, whether it is a support group for new employees, recently divorced employees, working mothers, or single fathers, step up and offer yourself as a leader.

5. *Get involved in or start a neighborhood group.*

   The best way to improve the beauty and safety of a neighborhood is to bring all of the residents together to focus on their common interests. It can also give you the opportunity to practice and develop leadership, organizational, and communication skills outside the office setting while doing something to benefit your community.

6. *Join your local Chamber of Commerce and get involved in committees or projects in your field of interest.*

   If you have an interest in learning more about the businesses and business leaders in your town, the local Chamber or the Convention and Visitors Bureau is always looking for dynamic and skilled volunteers to help with community events and programs. Often you will be dealing with top executives in local businesses, and they are always on the lookout for individuals who can add value to their companies.

7. *Get involved in city government.*

Politics and government are not for everyone, but if you have an interest in public service, there are ample opportunities to display your talents on any of a vast array of boards, committees, and special events. Whether your interests are in the field of accounting, construction, recreation, legal affairs, politics, or the inner workings of government, City Hall offers you the chance to show what you can do.

8. *Become a regular guest commentator on local radio or television.*

Child care therapists, veterinarians, gardeners, auto mechanics, computer wizards, coaches, legal experts, financial advisers, stockbrokers, and pediatricians and other physicians are among those who have benefited from heightened visibility by providing their services as a commentator, columnist, or regular guest on local media. If you have an area of expertise that lends itself to this outlet, I'd recommend that you offer your services at no charge as a benefit to the community. If you have something worthwhile to offer, you will reap ample benefits from the added exposure.

9. *Write guest editorials or regular letters to the editor for your local newspaper.*

Newspaper studies have shown that the letters to the editor and guest editorials are among the most-read sections of newspapers. This is a good way to offer the value of your expertise, informed opinions, and concerns. It is not a good place to rant, criticize, or take potshots at your neighbors. A thoughtful, well-reasoned, and well-written guest editorial can add to both the value of your Life Brand and to the welfare of your community.

10. *Teach a course at your local university or community college.*

Like most of the suggestions here, this one doesn't come with the promise of much financial reward, but by offering your knowledge and experience to others, you can add greatly to the value of others' lives and expand your success circles at the same time. I can't tell you how much I have enjoyed my teaching and lecturing experience. I don't mind telling you that I've probably learned as much, if not more, than the bright young people in my classes. I strongly urge you to offer your services as a teacher, role model, and mentor if it appeals to you at all as an outlet for your talents.

11. *Publish a book or a guide.*

There are few things as challenging and rewarding as publishing a book or guide in your field of interest. You shouldn't go into it trying to write a best-seller, however. Your goal should be to pack as much value into its pages as the publisher will allow, because a book has a long, long life. Unlike a speech, it's not there and then gone. You want to write it so that you can be proud when your children and grandchildren pick it up to show it to their children and grandchildren. Having a book published offers a level of credibility that is difficult to attain in any other way, and it is a wonderful opportunity to offer your Life Brand assets to a wide audience.

12. *Give free presentations at conferences or workshops.*

Developing an expertise within your profession or community and offering to conduct workshops or presentations at conferences is a great way to stand out. Offering free seminars is more likely to win you media coverage, while giving you a reputation as someone who is service-oriented and willing to provide something of value to others. Whether it is gardening tips, basic investment education, computer training, or motivational training, offering your services without charge is a great way to build a base audience and to increase your visibility.

13. *E-mail articles or send information of interest to bosses or coworkers, friends and family, and community leaders.*

Information is the greatest currency today, and if you can develop a reputation as a gatekeeper who provides useful information, it can only help extend the reach of your brand. Be aware of what interests those around you, and when you come across information that might be useful to them e-mail or send it to them with a "news you can use" note. Don't overdo it and don't ask for anything in return. Your rewards will come eventually.

14. *Start an advisory board for your business or organization, inviting industry leaders or other knowledgeable sources to be your mentors.*

I did this with Athletes Against Drugs and I've done it also in my business ventures. Most successful people are extremely busy, but most are also open to giving advice and guidance. If you are straightforward and don't place great demands on their time, most people are willing to offer the benefit of their experience and to share their networks if they believe in what you are doing.

15. *Start a top-ten list in your field.*

I'm told that Mr. Blackwell, the keeper of the infamous "Worst Dressed" list, was not a well-known designer until he began issuing annual citations for fashion folly. His annual list of the "worst dressed" is now as much a part of life

161

as Groundhog Day. Personally, I think it is better to take the high road, as Faye Childs did. How about putting together a "Best of . . ." list for your hometown giving the best hot dog stand, best bicycle shop, best bookstore, and so on? Or you might do a top-ten list for your professional or hobby organization in order to raise your profile.

16. *Get on the grade school, college, or high school lecture tour.*

Young audiences are both forgiving and a great test market. They aren't afraid to ask questions, which can only help sharpen your skills. By taking your presentations to the schools you also build a base audience. College and high school students will be out in the real world in just a few years, and teachers are known for spreading the word in their communities and within their profession. I've known many entertainers, public speakers, and others who have developed both their skills and their target audience on the school circuit.

17. *Apprentice yourself to a mentor or role model.*

There is no greater compliment you can pay an accomplished person than to approach him or her humbly and politely and say, "I would like to learn from you." Even those with little time to spare find it difficult to turn down someone with that request. If the person simply has no time to spend with you, ask if you can work for little or no pay in order to "shadow" and simply learn from being around the individual. I have benefited from several wonderful mentors, and in some cases I worked for them at little or no salary simply in order to observe them up close and learn. You may not be invited into the inner circle right away, or ever, but if nothing else, in making the request you introduce yourself to someone who may one day be willing to share experiences and knowledge with you.

18. *Become "everybody's favorite volunteer" at work, at home, and in the community.*

    This is a particularly effective way for young people to increase their visibility and brand value. You may not have experience. You may not have a lot of knowledge in your field. But you do have time and energy, two assets that you should not undervalue. By volunteering to do the tough and time-consuming tasks at work, in your relationships, and in the community, you can build a brand image as someone who gets things done, and that is a very valuable asset. I've also known senior citizens who have enriched their own lives and done great things in their community by serving as enthusiastic volunteers in their retirement years.

19. *Create a Web site for your Life Brand.*

    It is estimated that by the year 2005 about 720 million people around the globe will regularly use the Internet. Major brand companies like Gap, Dell Computer, Jaguar, Office Depot, and others have greatly increased their businesses by offering online shopping, while many others such as amazon.com and CDNow do business only online. It's been predicted that within the next decade, individual Web sites will be nearly as common as individual telephone numbers.

    If there was ever any doubt as to the power of the Internet for marketing personal brands, I think it has been proved beyond a doubt by people like Martha Stewart and even Matt Drudge. He was an unknown, untrained commentator and gossip writer who has become a highly paid media star as the result of the "Drudge Report," his online column that, for better or worse, has not only carried his version of the news but made news too. Some have complained that Drudge has played fast and loose with the truth, but there is no arguing that he has successfully expanded his brand on the Internet. He is by no means alone.

How many former U.S. Surgeons General can you name? I'm sure the only one most people can come up with is Dr. C. Everett Koop, who became an eighty-two-year-old Web phenom when he launched his medical advice Web site drkoop.com in 1999 and then took his Web-based company public at $9.00 a share and watched it soar to $16 and higher, reaping millions for Dr. Koop and other investors. Internet stock analysts noted that while the company itself was unproved, it was involved in the hot and growing market of online health. It was also frequently noted that the company and the Web site would benefit from the strong credibility (the Life Brand) of Dr. Koop, an esteemed pediatric surgeon and health advocate. When Dr. Koop's new Internet health care site formed an alliance with Internet giant America Online, *The New York Times* noted, "The four-year agreement gives AOL a link to a widely respected name in medicine . . ."

That's a key point. Anyone can build a Web site these days. It's the value you bring to it that will determine whether or not it becomes a standout. Today, politicians, performers, professionals, and just regular folks are using the Web to expand their brands in their work, their relationships, and their communities. It's a great way to market and expand your Life Brand by presenting your talents, interests, points of view, knowledge, skills, and expertise to millions and millions of Web surfers. Others who have seen the light and expanded their brands on Web sites include:

o Jesse Ventura. In his successful campaign to become the governor of Minnesota, former pro wrestler Ventura raised money, organized volunteers, and reached out to voters from his Web site, saving millions of dollars in campaign costs.

o *The Blair Witch* producers. In 1997, two thirty-year-old film school graduates and horror movie buffs made an eighty-seven-minute video in which the actors improvised the story as they went along. They took their film, which they entitled *The Blair Witch Project,* to the Sundance Film Festival thinking that, at best, they might sell it to a cable network programmer or a video producer. Instead, their unusual project became a cult hit at Sundance and won a $1 million deal with a small independent movie distributor. To get the word out about their movie, the filmmakers had created a Web site.

   With limited funds available for marketing the movie, the distributor, Artisan Entertainment, decided to expand the Web site to include more video clips. They also took the unusual step of advertising the Web site in a full-page advertisement in *Variety.* As word spread from Sundance to horror movie fans around the country, that Web site became one of the most popular on the Internet. Before the movie even hit theaters, there had been more than 11.5 million visitors to the site. When *The Blair Witch Project* proved to be the surprise hit of the summer of 1999, the use of the Web site to market the film was credited for much of its success.

o Rock singer Meredith Brooks. She uses her Web site, meridithbrooksrocks.com, to communicate directly with her fans. She posts audio and video clips of songs in progress on the site to get early feedback and makes decisions on what to include in her albums based on what her fans say.

o Stephen W. Bullington. You might think the obscure profession of "consulting entomologist" wouldn't lend itself to an alluring Web site. But Bullington, of Falls Creek, Pennsylvania, has expanded his career brand with his Forensic Entomology Web site, which offers information to police on how insects can be used to estimate a murder victim's time of death. He has another Web site that offers assistance and information to amateur bug collectors.

There are a multitude of free or very inexpensive services and software to help you launch your own Web site. This may be the best tool ever available for individuals to expand their Life Brands in their businesses, in their relationships, and in the communities they wish to reach. Don't miss out. Computer prices are cheaper than they ever have been, and if you still cannot afford one, there are now cyber-coffeehouses and other businesses that provide them to you for relatively low costs. Your local library may also offer the use of computers and Internet access at little or no fee.

Here are a few tips for this cutting-edge tool for marketing and expanding your Life Brand:

o Don't be shy. A personal Web site offers an incredible opportunity to let the world know the value you represent. Whether you are trying to hook up with people of similar interests, hoping to establish yourself as an expert in your field, or merely hoping to entertain visitors with your wit and wisdom, let it all hang out. There have been scores of cases where personal Web sites have opened up unexpected opportunities for their owners, so don't miss out by failing to be honest, open, and unembarrassed.

o Don't lie. Stretching the truth, lying about your credentials, or boasting that you can bench press 350 pounds when you can barely raise an eyebrow won't do you or your Life Brand any good. Stick with the real you and emphasize the real value you have to offer the world.

o Think of your Web site visitors as friends. Invite them into your home and tell them about your life, your entire life. You let your friends in on your work, your personal life, your dreams, and your frustrations. You can share those with Web visitors too. Use an informal, conversational "voice" and don't be afraid to let them know you are human. I've heard of people who thought their Web sites were "mostly personal" but they've attracted job offers because recruiters were impressed with the individual's attitude or creativity. Keep that in mind.

o Offer helpful, entertaining, or exotic links on your Web site. Even if you don't think of yourself as an expert source on any given topic, you can enhance your brand by helping connect others to sources of information. One of the reasons Matt Drudge's Web site became popular was that he offered direct links to the Web sites of dozens of newspapers, wire services, and columnists in both the United States and Europe.

The Internet is now bursting with personal brand Web sites that offer links to other Web sites offering information on everything from jobs to college costs to antique cars and the latest information on the Dixie Chicks. Once again, the best way to build your Life Brand is to offer value, and in today's world, nothing is more valued than information. By setting up a Web site that provides useful or unusual links to things you are interested in, you provide a service to people of similar interests, you build a network, and you add value to your own brand. But make sure you check frequently to ensure that those links are all up-to-date and still functional. There's nothing worse than sending a Web site visitor off on a wild-goose chase.

# The Power of Your
# Life Brand at Work

## CHAPTER EIGHT

> This is the true joy in life, the being used for a purpose
> recognized by yourself as a mighty one; the being a force of
> nature instead of a feverish, selfish little clod of ailments and
> grievances complaining that the world will not devote itself to
> making you happy. I want to be throughly used up when I die,
> for the harder I work the more I live.
>
> —GEORGE BERNARD SHAW

IN THE SPRING of 1999, Brian Ramey, thirty-one, and
Michelle Bucuk, twenty-nine, were a couple of newly minted
net entrepreneurs wondering how they were ever going to get
their business off the ground. They had worked together at
R. R. Donnelley, the giant printing firm based in Chicago.
Michelle is a Web designer. Brian is a graphic designer. Neither had worked at Donnelley more than a couple years when
they decided to jump into the entrepreneurial market with a
new company, Parking Karma (a name inspired by many fruit-
less hours in search of a city parking spot). Their goal was to
use their talents to create innovative, attractive, and exciting
Web sites for other entrepreneurs and established businesses.

They got off to a slow start. So slow that Michelle was
prepared to take a full-time job in order to be able to work
part-time for their company. Then, one day that summer,
something strange and wonderful happened in the city of

Chicago. Delightfully dressed cows began appearing on sidewalks around the city—more than 300 cows of a type never before seen in barnyards, stockyards, or farm pastures. They were fiberglass "art" cows created by artists as part of a public art project entitled "Cows on Parade."

Brian was captivated by the cows. He thought they were an exciting addition to the city and he wanted to tell his friends and family back in his hometown, Crawfordsville, Indiana, about them. "I tried to describe them to people, but they just thought I was crazy. Since a picture is worth a thousand words, I started scanning photographs of the cows into my computer and e-mailing them to people. Soon, they were forwarding my pictures of cows to other people and I started getting requests for more of them. It got pretty crazy," said Brian.

Excited by the response, Brian called Michelle and suggested that they put together a Web site for friends and family members. Their www.artcows.com Web site was incredibly well done. It offered not only photographs of each and every cow but also the name of the artist and sponsor, maps, and links to related Web sites. "We thought it might interest a few hundred people in Chicago and our relatives and friends, no big deal," said Michelle. "But in the first six weeks, the site had more than 8 *million* visitors."

The first Web site put together by the two-person shop at Parking Karma proved to be one of the hottest of the summer on the Internet. Yahoo.com named it a "Pick of the Week." *USA Today* selected it as a "hot site." And soon, reporters and potential customers were flooding Brian and Michelle with phone calls and e-mails.

"We've had inquiries from a couple of advertising agencies, a television station, a catering company, a software company, and the city of Chicago about doing Web sites for them," said Michelle.

"We created it just for fun, but we've had nothing but positive feedback from people and it's generated a lot of interest in our company," noted Brian. "We've had some companies call and want to put banner advertisements on the site but we don't want to do anything to spoil the integrity of the art project. We don't want any hard sell, so we've resisted doing any advertising, except for the city's literacy program, on the site."

Both Brian and Michelle understand the concept of branding. They think it's a good idea for entrepreneurs to market their brands on the Internet. But they hadn't given any thought to marketing their own brand when they started their ArtCows Web site project; it just happened to work out that way.

"I think this worked out so well for us because we came at it from the point of view that we weren't looking for what it could do for us, we were simply trying to do something for other people that we thought they would enjoy," Brian said. "We've met an incredible network of people through this, including the artists who created the cows, people in advertising, photographers, and people with the city of Chicago. Our biggest goal now is to build relationships with them that will be good for all of us for a long time."

## THE FREE AGENT NATION

Brian and Michelle have plugged into a network of entrepreneurs who are part of a rapidly developing trend that business analysts and media call the "Free Agent Nation." The Department of Labor estimates that 7.5 million people, roughly one in every sixteen workers, are self-employed independent contractors, freelancers, or "solo-preneurs." Others have estimated the number of free agents at twice that figure, saying it should include 2.3 million temporary workers and millions more of those who may work for someone else by day but also have "side jobs" that bring in additional income. *American Demographics* magazine reports that the number of home businesses grows by 2 million each year, and the Bureau of Labor Statistics says the number of Americans who describe themselves as self-employed rose 15 percent between 1997 and 1998. It is really difficult to get a handle on how many free agents are out there, but I do know that the Internal Revenue Service has been mailing out more than 74 million copies of Form 1099-MISC—the form used by self-employed people—which has been called "the pay stub of free agents."

## NEW APPROACHES TO WORK AND LIFE

The explosion in the free agent market is one of my primary inspirations for writing this book to encourage you to develop a Life Brand. The growing trends in self-employment, home-based businesses, outsourcing, and entrepreneurship within corporations has made it all the more important for individuals to identify their unique assets and to manage themselves as "brands" in the marketplace.

Across the nation and around the world, more and more men and women are creating their own free agent businesses built around their skills and passions. Even those who work in a corporate environment increasingly are encouraged to think of themselves as free agents within the company. They are defining their own jobs, creating their own projects, and acting as entrepreneurs in their areas of responsibility and expertise. A well-defined, ever-expanding, and wisely marketed brand is essential, then, for anyone hoping to stand out in today's highly competitive, fast-changing labor market.

The Free Agent Nation is a brand builder's paradise. In today's workplace, whether you are self-employed or working for a giant corporation, it pays dividends to develop, build, market, and expand your personal brand. "Now, more than ever, people are responsible for inventing their own careers . . . And for your brand to endure, it has to be tested, redefined, managed and expanded as markets evolve. Brands either learn or disappear," branding consultant Lisa Gansky of Marketect told *Fast Company*.

Computer technology and the Internet, a new emphasis on family and "quality" lifestyles, and a booming economy have led to more and more people striking out on their own by developing a clearly defined brand identity, marketing it, and always looking for opportunities to expand it. The National Association of the Self-Employed reports that it now has more than 300,000 members, many of whom are part of the hot SOHO, or single operator home office, market that has become a primary marketing target of credit card companies, office furniture makers, and office supply stores.

The signs of the flourishing free agent market are all around us. Some of them say "Kinko's" or "Sir Speedy." Others say "Federal Express" or "United Parcel." Office supply superstores, which have flourished because of the free agent market, are packed full of products that are the tools of the trade for home offices and small businesses. Software such as *Quicken* and *File Maker Pro* enable free agents to manage their companies without having to hire in-house accountants or a stenographic pool to keep them organized.

A great deal of the entrepreneurial free agent growth has been fueled by the increased "outsourcing" of work by corporations to specialized businesses like Brian's and Michelle's Parking Karma. Tasks like graphic design, document management, public relations, bookkeeping, payroll, and others are frequently contracted out to smaller firms, many of them launched by people downsized by the very corporations that now use their services.

As big companies focus more on their core businesses, they look outside their ranks for specialists to handle their other needs. Some large companies like Xerox Business Services, which handles photocopying and mail room tasks, among other things, and like Paychex Inc., which operates payroll and retirement plans for its clients, have flourished by serving those needs. Smaller entrepreneurial companies have succeeded by finding their own highly specialized niches.

## THE BEST JOB SECURITY IS A LIFE BRAND THAT OFFERS VALUE AND SERVICE

The U.S. Bureau of Labor reports that the average employment tenure for traditional workers is now under five years, while the average free agent has been working independently for nearly eight years. With so many businesses being swallowed up by bigger companies or conglomerates—and so many of their employees then being downsized out of their jobs—free agents often claim that they feel more secure working on their own than for a large corporation. As corporate employees, their jobs are largely dependent on one company—their employer. With their own businesses, however, they can build up a wider base of customers or clients.

Social scientists say that fewer and fewer people entering the workforce today will have long-term careers with any one company. In the twenty-first century, the old "career ladder" will all but disappear. The typical career path will more likely resemble a rock climb, in which you progress by testing the footing of many alternate routes, zigzagging your way to the top rather than following the traditional straight-ahead approach.

For those who build Life Brands of high quality, the sky is the limit in this environment. Whether you draw a paycheck from a big company, a small business, or from your own home-based operation, you should take responsibility for managing and marketing yourself as a business or product in a marketplace that is subject to rapid change. "People with the right combination of savvy and ambition can afford to shop for the right boss, the right colleagues, the right environment," noted former U.S. Secretary of Labor Robert B. Reich in an interview.

One of the really interesting things about the growth in free agents is that they seem to be happy in their freedom. Eighty-four percent of the independent workers surveyed by the Bureau of Labor Statistics said they preferred being free agents over working for someone else. They seem extremely secure too. More than 96 percent of them believe they could continue happily in their arrangement as long as they wish.

I've come to know a great many people like Brian and Michelle in recent years, and the one thing that stands out about all of them is that while they are passionate about what they do, they don't let their work define them. Instead, they define their work. These free agents have highly marketable skills or knowledge that draws others to their brands. Those unique talents and personal traits are their Life Brand *assets*. They develop them. They market them. They manage them. And they are continually working to add to their value because they do what they do not out of necessity but out of passion.

The explosion in free agents has also set off a wave of creativity in the world of small business. Once people are free to express their talents, they tend to create innovative ways to make a living from them. Many free agents have found the Internet to be ripe ground for their creativity, but not all of them are high-tech entrepreneurs. One of the more interesting free agent success stories I've heard is that of Marc Friedland.

As a boy, Marc enjoyed writing letters to his friends on unusual objects, including motion sickness bags taken from commercial airlines. Even while he was studying for his degrees in psychology and public health, he'd design unique greeting cards as gifts for friends. Although he had planned to go to medical school, his greeting cards were so popular that friends encouraged him to open his own studio.

In the early 1980s, he began working out of an apartment in West Los Angeles, crafting invitations and greeting cards out of tree leaves or Alka-Seltzer packets. In 1986, he moved to a studio office and picked up his first celebrity client, actor Dudley Moore, who hired him to do birthday party invitations after seeing invitations Friedland had done for the Museum of Contemporary Art in Los Angeles.

Today, his company, Creative Intelligence, has twenty-five employees and annual sales of about $2 million. His clients include many of the biggest names in show business, business executives, and other affluent people willing to pay as much as

$200 for a single wedding invitation. In addition, Friedland also sells his custom stationery and envelopes, which retail for $800 per 100, through Neiman-Marcus and Bergdorf Goodman. As a free agent, he has created such a powerful brand that even *People* magazine took notice. "This is my hobby, and it is my life," Friedland told its reporter. "It really is a business based on passion."

Like Marc Friedland, I believe in pursuing my passions and then identifying ways to profit from them. If you are a professional care-giver, does it matter if it's a state or private agency or your own business that issues your paycheck? It won't if your primary concern is helping people deal with problems. If you are an architect or a master carpenter, is your loyalty to your boss or is it to your craft? Certainly you want to work for the best company in the most comfortable environment where the opportunities are the greatest, but mostly you want to do what you love to do. Why shouldn't you?

## BRAND-BUILDING FREE AGENTS THRIVE WITHIN CORPORATE AMERICA TOO

It's possible to be happy and fulfilled working for others too, of course. CEOs, middle managers, and line employees are all finding that the old "command and control" model of management is too rigid and unwieldy for today's fast-moving global business world. To break down the walls, open up communication, and increase creativity, companies of all sizes are asking their people to build their individual brands and to approach their jobs as if they were the owners and operators of the business.

Many corporations now encourage their employees to think of themselves as free agents. They sense that it is better to have self-motivated and enthusiastic employees than insecure workers standing around waiting for instructions on what to do next and how to do it.

In 1993, Chris Turner of Xerox Business Services was given the job of rejuvenating and uniting the corporate culture at one of the fastest-growing companies in the nation. The goal of her acclaimed change program was to turn each and every one of the company's 15,000 employees into a free-thinking free agent. "We assumed that everyone wanted to be an entrepreneur within the company and we gave them credit for having the brains and initiative to do it," said Turner, who is now a free agent consultant and author.

## TURNING TALENTS AND PASSIONS INTO OPPORTUNITIES

Just as the unique style of a Marc Friedland party invitation, a Donna Karan suit, and the flavor of Starbucks Coffee are distinctive assets that set them apart, so are the special blends of talents, knowledge, and characteristics that are packaged in the personal brand that bears *your* name. Friedland is always looking for ways to expand his brand into new markets. Donna Karan's top executives make sure they do all they can to keep improving, expanding, and marketing their brand's assets to add value. Starbucks has been wildly successful at doing the same. How about you?

It is critical that you develop your unique Life Brand assets, not just for your financial success but for your mental, social, and spiritual health. You have been given gifts. It is up to you to develop them and market them as your Life Brand. If you don't, you risk being left behind by those free agents who have already seen the light.

The Internet has helped millions of free agents develop and market their Life Brands in the workplace. Among the Web sites devoted to brand-conscious self-employed men and women are Freeagent.com and Aquent's Talent Finder, which both offer group rate packages for health and dental insurance, tax services, lawyers, and other benefits that are usually available to corporate employees. Another hot Internet site for free agents looking for either contract or full-time employment is the Monster Talent Market, the world's first auction house for free agents. The creators of Monster.com claim to have more than 230,000 job listings from more than 30,000 employers.

You can go to the Web site at Monster.com, fill out an in-depth form describing your unique brand assets, list the geographical locations where you are willing to work, how much you want to be paid, and devise a brand slogan like "the Deck Doctor." You then put your services up for a five-day auction. If you are hired, the employer pays Monster.com a fee in the $250 to $1,000 range, depending on how much you are getting paid.

The Monster Talent Market opened on July 6, 1999, and on the first day, 9,010 free agents put themselves up for hire. Among those who jumped on the block were database administrators, consultants of all kinds, as well as free agents offering their services as dog-bite experts, tuba and guitar instructors, a clown, car salesmen, oil field workers, lawyers, and an Elvis impersonator specializing in delivering "E-grams." By late 1999, Monster.com had 70,000 registered contractors and about 5,000 registered employers, with 20,000 ongoing auctions.

Entrepreneurial employees never stop building their brands by learning new skills and expanding their expertise so that they can "sell" their services to the highest bidder whether it is within the company or outside it. Rob Steir, thirty-four, an MBA from Northwestern University's Kellogg Graduate School of Management, recognized this trend early on. He founded MBA FreeAgents in New York in 1996 after growing bored with his career in commercial real estate. Initially, he thought he'd look for a job in the hot Internet market but the headhunter he signed up with didn't give the sort of service he wanted. Sensing that there was a market that was not being served, he established his own job-finding business for people with similar qualifications. MBA FreeAgents soon had a database containing more than 3,400 names, which companies could access for an upfront fee of $495. If a company hires someone listed on MBA FreeAgents' site to serve as a consultant or to work on a special project, it pays Steir's firm between $1,500 and $2,500, depending on the length of the term of service.

A similar organization, M Squared, which launched in 1988, has worked with more than 600 companies, most of them Fortune 500 members. It helps clients find free agents to work on projects ranging from setting up human resources departments to helping with mergers. M Squared takes a cut of a worker's hourly fee or a percentage of the total project fee. "Companies used to ask, 'Who are these people and why don't they have real jobs?' recalled M Squared vice president Lori Perlsdtadt in a *New York Times* report. "Now free agency is everywhere."

Even top business executives have joined the free agent

wave. Werner von Pein, fifty-seven, was a senior executive in the food industry for thirty years at companies such as Procter & Gamble, Quaker Oats, and General Foods, but after being caught up in several downsizings, he joined the free agent market. He became one of the "temp executives" dispatched by Executive Interim Management. According to a report in *The Wall Street Journal*, Pein and other free agent business leaders with Executive Interim Management generally earn $1,000 to $1,500 a day filling in for companies that have a hole at the top, or doing the dirty work that a company's own executives don't want to touch. Pein told *The Wall Street Journal* that after being downsized so many times himself, he decided that rather than fight the downsizing trend, he'd capitalize on it. "Mentally, I've said there's no guarantee anyway, so I might as well do something I enjoy," he noted.

## WHAT YOU DO FOR A LIVING IS PART OF WHO YOU ARE

This trend in free agency is also the result of the breakdown in the old barriers separating our personal and professional lives. In the not-so-distant past, your fathers and mothers often felt that they had to separate who they *were* from what they *did*. People had separate brands for their personal and professional lives. In that environment, you often heard people say things like, "You have to get to know her outside the office; she's really a good person." In the workplace, people were not encouraged to display family photographs, to talk about family concerns, or to take time off for family matters. It just wasn't considered "businesslike."

Today, it is important to build a Life Brand that reflects a balance among work, relationships, and community life. More and more, companies encourage and expect their employees to take time for family activities and community service. Business leaders have come to understand that stable relationships and commitment to community are the hallmarks of reliable, long-term employees. That's why family leaves are increasingly common and flex-time is widely accepted. Many employers allow their people to work from home several days a week. Some even encourage it. And it is not at all unusual to see parents bring their children into the office. Businesses also are giving their employees time off and other support so they can do community service in the belief that everyone should be an active part of the larger community.

## IT'S NOT WHERE YOU WORK, IT'S WHAT YOU DO

With the new emphasis on maintaining a balance between your work and your private life, it is important to build balance into your Life Brand. For your own mental and spiritual health, you want to have a brand that is valued by those you love and respect, and valued also within the communities that you are a part of. This is not just a work-related issue. Building a quality Life Brand will have a tremendous impact on every aspect of your existence. Very simply, it is a way to establish who you want to be and how you want to be perceived while you are here, and after you've gone.

Brian and Michelle and all the others in their freelance

network have worked not only to master their particular areas of expertise but also to stand out in their fields. One of the best ways to do that is to serve not only your customers or clients but your community too. To attract clients and to build mutually beneficial alliances with other strong Life Brands, you have to bring a lot to the table, you have to show integrity, *and* you have to have an identity that sets you apart from the competition. More and more people are realizing that it's not *where* you work that is important, it's *what you do* that matters.

Net entrepreneurs Brian and Michelle found a way to do what they love and make a living at it. They were willing to take risks to become free agents in order to get more satisfaction from their work, and their enthusiasm rubs off on everyone around them. The more time they spend building value into their brands, the more connections they'll make with potential clients.

# The Power of Your Life Brand in Your Relationships

CHAPTER NINE

**STEFANIE BELCHER MET** her future husband, Chris, when they were both teenagers living in northeastern Ohio. She was fifteen. He was two years older. They were an odd match. He was a big, rough guy. She was refined and delicate. After their first dance at a school party, they talked for hours and hours. They were never apart after that. They went to the same college, and married after graduation.

A few years later, they started a family. They had two children, and Stefanie devoted herself to them and to her husband. Chris's job forced him to be away from the family for weeks at a time. They also had to move a lot. According to Chris, one of Stefanie's great brand assets over the early years of their marriage was her willingness to make sacrifices for him and their family. "For ten years, our entire lives had been about me. My career came first, always," Chris told an interviewer. "Stefanie made every sacrifice in the world to support me, unconditionally. I would call her up and say, 'Okay, we're moving to Buffalo now,' and she would never complain . . . She's always been there for me."

184

Her willingness to unselfishly serve the needs of her family were part of Stefanie's Life Brand. She invested her assets in their lives as a wife and mother. She devoted herself to them. And when she was needy, she reaped the rewards of her investment. They gave her their love and support. She earned back her investment with interest when, in July 1998, doctors found a particularly deadly form of cancer in her right breast.

They told Stefanie that they would have to remove her breast and put her through many weeks of chemotherapy. As soon as he learned of his wife's cancer, Chris announced that he was quitting his job so that he could stay home and take care of her. "What kind of husband would I be if I didn't drop everything for Stefanie when she got sick? Did I want her sister to have to hold her hand while she suffered because I wasn't there? Did I want Stefanie's mother to have to sit with her in the hospital while they were shooting needles into her and filling her up with those awful chemicals, or did I want to be there myself? Did I want some neighbor to have to tell my children why Mommy's hair was falling out all over the place? No. This is my family. This is my responsibility. This is my home. This is my duty . . ." he told a magazine interviewer.

Serving her family had always been Stefanie's priority. She gave them love and support and they returned it when her cancer was diagnosed. In telling you about Stefanie and Chris so far I've left out some information because I didn't want to distract you from my basic point. But in some ways, it makes this couple's story all the more compelling. Stefanie's husband is Chris Spielman, who is widely considered to be one of the strongest and most ferocious linebackers in the National Football League. His job was starting at linebacker for the Buffalo Bills of the NFL.

Chris quit his job and gave up the sport he loved because

his wife had always been there to support him in his career. He took over her duties with the children, supervised them, fed them, played with them, and tucked them in. He also became Stefanie's primary caregiver. He fed her and helped her through the chemotherapy. When she lost all of her hair, he shaved his head.

Stefanie's cancer is in remission now. She is back home taking care of her family. Chris returned to playing football briefly for the Cleveland Browns, where he was once again regarded as one of the NFL's top linebackers, and retired from competitive play in August 1999. At home, however, his Life Brand represents something much different. He is a loving husband and father who gives at least as much as he gets from his relationships. He understands the importance of being there for those who have been there for him.

## TAKING CARE NOT TO TAKE OTHERS
## FOR GRANTED

What is the value of a Life Brand when it comes to relationships? As in the case of your career or work life, building a Life Brand helps you to focus on developing your assets and using them to build value for your "target market." The target market in your relationships, of course, is made up of the people you love and care most about. Your rewards are not career success, material goods, or wealth. They are the love and friendships that fill your heart and nourish your soul.

Too often, we take our relationships for granted. We don't invest the same thought, time, and energy in maintaining them as we do in building our careers or pursuing other interests. We think love or familiarity is enough. It isn't. Love is a powerful force, but love doesn't live or grow in a vacuum. To keep love alive, you have to feed it with a rich supply of consideration, loyalty, trustworthiness, sensitivity, thoughtfulness, cooperation, compromise, tolerance, and responsibility.

Have you ever gone to a loved one, or a friend, for support in a time of crisis or challenge and received an indifferent or a negative response? Could it be that you went to the well without priming the pump? It might have been because you did not put enough into that relationship to expect anything out of it. In difficult times, we lean on our relationships for strength and support. If you haven't invested in the welfare of the people around you, it's not very realistic to expect them to take an interest in you and your problems, is it?

Stefanie Spielman poured all of her skills, knowledge, and energy, as well as her love and devotion, into raising her children, supporting her husband, and creating a nurturing home for them. Everything that she poured out, they returned. For all of his exterior toughness and his great love of his sport, Chris did not give a second thought to leaving football when his wife and children needed him. He devoted himself to Stefanie because she had invested so much love in their relationship.

## A SOLID FOUNDATION BUILT UPON MUTUAL SUPPORT

Taking a relationship for granted is as foolish as taking a job for granted. You simply can't afford to coast in either. The more effort you put into them, the more you can expect to get out of them. When you build a Life Brand, it helps you stay focused on the importance of relationships in your life. It makes you more aware of your responsibility to serve the needs of others by using your assets to enhance the value of their lives. If you think of your loved ones, your friends, your coworkers, and others around you as your "target market" and take every opportunity to do that, you will likely build lasting and supportive relationships.

Stephen Covey offers a powerful metaphor for the art of building mutually beneficial relationships. In his book *The 7 Habits of Highly Effective People,* he writes about creating "emotional bank accounts" for the people in your life, then making sure that you make more deposits than withdrawals into their accounts. You make a *deposit* when you do something for people, whether it is simply paying them a compliment or helping them work through a problem. You make a *withdrawal* when you ask them for a favor, or when you somehow demand more of them than you are giving back. Stephen encourages his readers to make more deposits than withdrawals into the emotional bank accounts of the people they care about. By building up these "deposits," you then will be welcome to make withdrawals from the relationship when you need support.

The strongest Life Brands are those built on a foundation of mutually supportive and long-term relationships. In some cases, those relationships are between spouses, sometimes they are between friends, children, or siblings, and even among people who work together or those who share community ties. Each relationship has its unique aspects. The one common denominator is trust. It is the air that relationships breathe. Without it, relationships cannot survive.

# TRUSTWORTHINESS IS A VITAL COMPONENT OF ANY LIFE BRAND

Your ability to work with others and to bond with them quickly is crucial to your long-term success and happiness. Trust is essential if other people are to share their knowledge, skills, and connections with you. How do you establish your Life Brand as one that is worthy of trust? I'm not going to give you a list of ten ways to win friends and influence people. I'm afraid there are no shortcuts to creating trust between two people. No tricks—no pat phrases, gestures, or facial expressions that will win you the lasting trust of others. You have to earn it by showing that you are trustworthy. You have to walk the talk.

## Seven Keys to Building Trustworthiness

1. *Learn to see others as the product of their experiences, not yours.*
   It is human nature to try to understand other people based on our own feelings, emotions, and histories. It is wrong to always expect others will act the way you would act, or that they will be interested in the same things you are interested in. Anyone who has ever raised more than one child knows that people do not respond the same way even to the same environment or the same parenting techniques.

   How do you come to any meaningful understanding of others? By listening to them as you would want them to listen to you. That means listening without judging or filtering their words through your own experiences. It means allowing others to express themselves so thoroughly that you can see the world from their perspective too. Once you stop talking, you'll be amazed at all you hear.

2. *Find common goals and work on them first.*

   One of the best ways to build trust is to focus on a shared goal or vision. It works on a wide range of levels. When there is a global disaster such as an earthquake, rescue workers from all over the world converge on the scene of devastation and they cooperate to help the victims. Even those people who may have long-standing disagreements over politics, religion, or other issues will work side by side under such circumstances. Why? Because cooperation is a basic part of human existence, whether you are talking about the way a great variety of cells act in harmony to form our bodies or the way in which drivers on the streets cooperate to keep the roads relatively safe by obeying traffic signs (most of the time).

3. *Communicate your feelings.*

   People form their impressions of you and your motives based on their own experiences and assumptions. If you want them to have a better understanding of you, then you need to communicate your feelings. You can't expect them to know what you want; you should tell them. Often, men and women have conflicts because one assumes that the other knows his or her needs and desires. Simple, honest communication can alleviate many of those conflicts. There is no cooperation without communication.

4. *Be a rock that others can depend upon.*

   Most people only have to review their own disappointments in life to realize the importance of this. Often the most hurtful experiences we go through occur when someone we have trusted, or wanted to trust, breaks a promise or refuses to honor a commitment. When it comes to building relationships, no promise is small enough to break. If you say you will do something, do it. If you can't do it, don't say you will. There is no greater way to earn trust than to live up to the expectations you set. *Everything* is a test when it comes to building trust.

5. *Live up to the standards that you demand of others.*

If you expect other people to honor you, then you have to honor all others in their presence. That means you don't say bad things about others who are not present. You don't lie or intentionally mislead anyone. It also means you act with integrity by setting high standards of personal behavior and then living up to them. Am I asking you to be a saint or to be overly righteous? No. I'm saying that you should model the integrity that you demand of others. If you can't live up to the expectations you set for others, then why should you be trusted? If you don't display honesty and integrity, how can you expect people to trust you or to give you what you don't offer them? If you demand that others fulfill their commitments, then you should fulfill yours.

6. *Acknowledge your mistakes, correct your errors, and be strong enough to apologize.*

It is one of the great flaws of our culture that so many people see it as a weakness to admit to a mistake or to apologize for mistreating another. In fact, it is the strong person who is willing to admit mistakes, correct errors, and apologize for bad behavior. It is very *strange* behavior, when you think about it, to always believe you are right or that your actions will always be benevolent. You and you alone? Or are we *all* always right?

If you accept that you are going to be wrong and that, at least occasionally, you are going to treat others poorly, it should not be all that hard to acknowledge errors and apologize for bad behavior. You certainly can't expect to win anyone's trust and cooperation by refusing to do so, can you? Often we fight, argue, and defend our actions as proper, but in fact they are wrong because we don't know the *whole* truth, or we don't understand the situation from the other person's perspective. There's an ancient Eastern verse that I think applies to those situations.

> *Granting that you and I argue.*
> *If you get the better of me, and not I of you,*
> *Are you necessarily right and I wrong?*
> *Or if I get the better of you and not you of me,*
> *Am I necessarily right and you wrong?*
> *Or are we both partly right and partly wrong?*
> *Or are both wholly right and wholly wrong?*
> *Since you and I cannot know,*
> *We all live in darkness*

7. *Understand that no one is required to give you trust; you are required to earn it.*

   If you are a product on a shelf of many similar products, what is it about you that I should trust more than any of the others? The packaging? The promise on the label? Your color and texture? All of these things may attract me to you, but the only true test is to see if you deliver on the promise by fulfilling the expectations. If you don't fulfill them—if you taste bad, or don't clean up the stain on the carpet, or fail to relieve my headache—then why should I ever come back to you?

   There is no reason. That is why it is important for you to remember always that others will buy into your Life Brand only if it delivers on its promise. Trust is earned, not granted. Trust and cooperation go hand in hand.

## FORM LIFE BRAND ALLIANCES THAT ENHANCE YOUR LIVES

Every individual I know with a powerful Life Brand enjoys strong bonds with people whose own Life Brands enhance and strengthen theirs. Good relationships can greatly enhance the quality of your life. Bad relationships can throw it into turmoil. Don't allow your Life Brand to be tarnished by negative people or anyone who doesn't bring out the best in you. I would also advise you not to form partnerships, personally or professionally, with anyone whose motives you suspect. You have to be every bit as vigilant about protecting your Life Brand image as consumer brands such as Pepsi, Tiffany, and Disney are about protecting their product images in the marketplace. You should be equally vigilant about building relationships that strengthen your brand.

The ability to build lasting relationships may be *the* most important Life Brand asset you will ever develop, personally or professionally. Increasingly, relationship skills are seen as vital in the workplace too. Business leaders have come to see corporations, suppliers, and clients as more like communities than machines, which was the old business model. The cultural dynamics of most businesses reflect the nature and the quality of the relationships within them. If the chief executive is a tyrant, then the culture reflects that, and often, so does the bottom line. While some CEOs have built Life Brands that reflect tough, even cutthroat approaches to management, they don't seem to hang on to their leadership positions very long. The men and women who succeed in business, and in life, are those who build mutually supportive relationships. They understand that creativity, responsiveness, and adaptability are maximized in a work culture in which people trust and support each other. If you can establish in your work, in your personal relationships, and in the greater community that you are willing to connect with others and to give more than you get, your Life Brand will stand out in everything you do.

Fay Vincent was forty years old, making $47,000 a year as a government lawyer, when he was offered the chance to become CEO and president of Columbia Pictures. "I knew nothing about business, disliked the movies, and occasionally wore brown shoes with a blue suit. I was not exactly Hollywood material," he told an interviewer. So why did he take the job? Because Vincent believes in making career decisions based on the quality of people he'll be working with. "Herb Allen, Columbia's major shareholder, had confidence in my abilities— which was a huge motivator," Vincent said. "It turned out to be the critical decision of my professional life."

## BUILDING CONNECTIONS THAT STRENGTHEN YOUR LIFE BRAND

How do you make connections that will enhance your Life Brand? You look for people whose Success Circles overlap with yours. Common goals and interests are catalysts for cooperative action that bring mutual benefits. The business world understands this more today than ever before. If you need evidence of that, simply take a look at all of the other brand-name companies that have tied their products in with the latest Disney movie. Or, when your next credit card bill comes in, note all of the other companies that are marketing their services with your card issuer.

As I write this, there is a mailing on my desk from the

AT&T Personal Rewards program that offers "200 terrific rewards choices" for points accrued by using AT&T's long-distance service. The rewards offered include free long-distance minutes with AT&T and special deals on AT&T products like designer telephones, answering machines, and cordless phones, but they also include discounts on products from companies that have no corporate ties to AT&T. With my AT&T reward points, I can get *The O'Jays' Greatest Hits,* gift certificates for product brands from Foot Locker, Gap, Home Depot, K-B Toys, Lands' End, Marriott, Macy's, United Artists Theaters, and *Newsweek,* among many others.

Why do all of those other big-brand companies offer discounts for an AT&T promotion? Because it also serves to extend the reach of *their* brands. All of those companies benefit from having their products included in marketing and promotional materials sent out by AT&T. It gives them increased exposure to AT&T's millions of loyal customers. Once those customers have used their reward points to sample those products, they may well become *their* loyal customers too. The same principles of brand association, cooperation, and strategic alliances hold true with your Life Brand.

## A NEW BUSINESS BUILT ON TRUST

One of the best business partnerships I've been involved in was born in the saddle of a very patient cutting horse, but it was built upon trust. I was herding cattle, believe it or not, as a guest at the Montana ranch of Grant Gregory, an investment banker and retired chairman of the accounting firm Touche Ross & Co., when I pitched the concept to my host.

I became acquainted with Grant when I joined him on

the board of directors of Junior Achievement, a worldwide organization founded in 1919 that works to educate and inspire young people by teaching them how the world of business and free enterprise works. I was asked to serve on the board of Junior Achievement to assist them in better understanding and communicating with youths.

In my dealings with the many top business executives who are associated with Junior Achievement, it struck me once again that most had very little knowledge of the urban marketplace or the buying habits of African-Americans, Hispanics, and other minorities. They didn't understand these other cultures because they had never been exposed to them up close. I thought that unfamiliarity was potentially harmful socially and economically for both sides. Socially, it's easier to discriminate against a racial group if you don't understand its people. Economically, I also felt that many businesses were missing the boat when it came to marketing their products and services to the rapidly expanding Hispanic and African-American middle classes. Black consumers have more than $500 billion in expendable income. Hispanics are the nation's fastest-growing ethnic group, and they are projected to be the largest minority group in the nation within a few short years.

With my marketing experience, I believed I was uniquely qualified to help companies reach these underserved but vast minority markets. Over several months, I developed a marketing action plan to pitch my company as a bridge to the African-American community. But before I made my pitch, I sharpened my skills and knowledge by researching the largest marketing and advertising firms and looking at what each of them was doing, or not doing, to help their clients reach minority consumers. I prepared myself for an opportunity, and in the mountains of Montana I came upon it.

I shared my observations and concerns with Grant Gregory as we rode on horseback over his beautiful ranch. The great scenery of the Old West must have had an impact, because Grant and I decided to do a little pioneering that day. He bought into my vision for creating a company that would open new frontiers in the multicultural market for America's biggest businesses. He offered to put me in touch with executives at one of the largest advertising and marketing firms in the country. He served on the board of directors of that company, and, as a man with a very powerful Life Brand, he had a great deal of influence that he graciously used on my behalf because he believed in what I was doing and he saw that we could establish a mutually beneficial alliance.

As a result, I am now a co-founder of New America Strategies Group, a New York–based network that provides strategic planning, marketing, consulting, and program development to companies seeking to reach multicultural consumers. Our mission is to build long-term loyalty between advertisers and multicultural audiences by creating programs and partnerships that have a positive impact on multicultural communities. NASG is a division of True North Communications, the sixth-largest advertising holding company in the world, with $1.2 billion in revenues and $11.2 billion in billings. True North employs 11,000 individuals in more than 300 offices worldwide. It has been a very rewarding partnership that has helped me extend my brand in many powerful ways. Through this partnership, I've developed business relationships with major clients such as Taco Bell, Bausch & Lomb, Merrill Lynch, Johnson & Johnson, and State Farm Insurance Co. I've worked to help those corporations and others reach new customers in multicultural markets, and I'd like to think many African-Americans, Hispanics, and others have benefited from that too. That was my vision, and Grant bought into it and supported it. With the trust and support of others, you can do anything. Without it, you will be just another brand on the shelf. Now, admittedly, my synergy with Grant happened at a high level. You may not have the opportunity to sit on the board of national service groups like Junior Achievement, where you can meet influential people such as Grant Gregory. But remember, I didn't start there either. It wasn't so long ago that I was working in management for the federal prison system. After that, I struggled for many years to establish my own sports marketing company. I had to work my way up the ladder just like everyone else, and the relationships that I've formed along the way have been invaluable.

## BECOME A LIFE BRAND LEADER BY BUILDING STRONG RELATIONSHIPS

One of the things I've noticed about people like Grant Gregory is that their relationship skills have made them natural leaders. Their ability to bring people of common interests together and build trust and cooperation quickly helps them accomplish tasks that otherwise might seem insurmountable. I was reminded of how relationship skills enhance a Life Brand when I met Alexis Herman. In 1999, the U.S. Department of Labor asked me to help it launch a program to prepare unemployed young people to join the workforce. Secretary of Labor Alexis M. Herman was concerned that too many young people in urban communities were not finding jobs. The program we launched is called the Youth Opportunity Movement, and it uses the resources of both the private sector and the government to help young men and women find meaningful employment.

In bringing this great program to reality, I couldn't help but be impressed by Secretary Herman, who is the first African-American, and only the fifth woman, to serve as Secretary of Labor. Secretary Herman has a powerful Life Brand, but more than that, she is a Life Brand leader. She stands out from even other quality Life Brands because of her remarkable ability to bring people together for the common good. She has built a fulfilling and meaningful life on a foundation of courage, integrity, trust, clear thinking, strong communication skills, and a deeply ingrained belief that everyone has the right to fair and equal treatment.

When Alexis Herman was a sophomore at Most Pure Heart of Mary Catholic High School in Mobile, Alabama, in the early 1960s, she became upset while watching the traditional crowning ceremony after the annual Christ the King parade. Taught by her parents to fight against injustice and discrimination, Alexis immediately confronted a church official and demanded to know why black students were never allowed to do the crowning. About six years later, after graduating from Xavier University in New Orleans, she returned to Mobile and took part in a successful campaign to desegregate the city's Catholic schools.

"Alexis is not somebody who's along for the ride," a White House aide once told *The New York Times.* "She's a highly principled person."

Life Brand leaders are great achievers who inspire others to achieve things that they might never be able to do as individuals. The world needs more of them, more leaders like Alexis Herman. People like you, for example. We need leaders of all types, all backgrounds, all skills, and all colors who can build the highest-quality Life Brands and then use their talents, skills, and knowledge to inspire others.

What is leadership? Philosophers, sociologists, and management gurus have been wrestling over one true definition for centuries. There are all sorts of leaders just as there are all sorts of followers. There are good leaders who have the best interests of their followers in mind, and there are bad leaders who promote their own agenda and interests above all others. Historian Doris Kearns Goodwin has written extensively about the leaders in American politics. Here is how she describes the leadership qualities of President John F. Kennedy in *Ten Lessons from Presidents*.

> [Kennedy] conveyed the most important sense that a leader can convey; that the problems of society, however large they might seem, can be solved by public action . . . Indeed, his strongest legacy was that he made young people feel that politics was an honorable profession and a rich adventure.

My definition of a Life Brand leader is someone who has the ability to inspire other people to take actions that serve the general good. While the profile may vary somewhat for leaders depending on their field—government, sports, church, family—I believe Life Brand leaders have the following characteristics:

o A clear vision of where they want to go and a plan for getting there
o They lead not because of their high rank or their power but because they build consensus and coalitions. People follow them because they *want* to, not because they *have* to.
o They are skillful negotiators. Rather than making demands,

they bring people together by first identifying common goals and then working toward them. "If you want to play the new career game, you have to be a good negotiator," Leigh Steinberg, a sports agent who represents NFL players Steve Young and Troy Aikman among others, told *Fast Company*. "It's not a natural skill. But for talented people in sports or business, this is a seller's market."

o They have strong two-way communication skills, listening as well as speaking.
o They have clearly defined principles that they consistently follow.
o They work well under pressure and handle stress effectively.
o They stand out because they are continually building more and more value into their Life Brands.

## THE POWER OF A LIFE BRAND LEADER

Take a walk through your local grocery store, Wal-Mart, or drugstore and note the thousands of brand-name products on the shelves. You will see many unfamiliar or lesser brands but there will be a few that stand out as brand leaders. There are many cola drinks on the market, but Pepsi and Coke are the dominant brands. There are scores of toothpastes, but how many brands can you name off the top of your head? Those too are the brand leaders. That's what you want to be—a Life Brand that stands above all others; one so powerful that your name is the first one people think of when they are looking for someone who does what you do, works where you work, lives where you live.

A leading brand consumer product is simply the one that

outsells all others because people believe it offers the greatest value. A Life Brand leader is a person with masterful relationship skills. They inspire others through their trustworthiness and their willingness to give without expecting anything in return. No one owns exclusive rights to leadership. The great leaders of history, politics, business, religion, law, and other fields have come from all walks of life and from all circumstances. We all have the power to become Life Brand leaders by following the example of dynamic people such as Alexis Herman, who has stretched her strong brand from social work to one of the highest positions in our federal government, and perhaps even beyond.

The daughter of a funeral home owner and a reading teacher, she grew up in the Deep South at a time when African-Americans were just beginning to rise up against the injustices of segregation and discrimination. Her parents taught leadership and character by their example. Her father was one of the first blacks elected as a ward leader in Alabama's Democratic Party organization after he successfully sued to enforce the right of African-Americans to vote in party elections. A courageous man, he once took his daughter's high school class on a field trip to observe a meeting of a hate group affiliated with the Ku Klux Klan. He wanted to teach Alexis and her classmates that racism was a real threat. They got the picture when whites at the meeting pelted them with boxes and cans.

After college, Alexis went to work for Catholic Charities, a social work organization devoted to helping people in need. She earned her reputation as a coalition builder in the trenches, at first in the shipyards of Pascagoula, Mississippi, where she convinced reluctant employers to offer more job opportunities to unskilled minority workers. In the early 1970s she moved to Atlanta, where she was successful in getting corporations to hire more college-educated minority women.

At this point, while still in Atlanta, Alexis stretched her talents, skills, and knowledge by moving also into the arena of politics, which would allow her to expand her brand by opening new opportunities. She participated in the winning mayoral campaigns of both Maynard Jackson and Andrew Young. Her abilities caught the attention of Georgia's Governor Jimmy Carter, who asked her to join the Labor Department as director of the women's bureau after he became president.

In the 1980s and 1990s, Alexis's reputation as a great organizer was established in political circles because of her involvement with the Democratic National Committee. As chief of staff, she organized the 1992 national convention. She moved to the White House in 1993 when President Clinton asked her to serve as head of the office of public liaison. She was responsible for "putting together coalitions around issues and sometimes smoothing over rough relations with key constituencies," reported *The Washington Post*.

In late 1996, the Clinton administration nominated her to replace outgoing Labor Secretary Robert Reich. Initially, she was not a popular choice with labor leaders, and even many Democrats preferred someone with higher levels of experience. Some worried that she had not had enough experience in the sorts of tough negotiations that often occur in labor disputes. But the president stood behind her, and Congress approved her nomination in May of 1997 after what some called the most intense battle that a Clinton cabinet nominee has faced.

All Life Brand leaders face challenges, and often their greatest tool is their ability to build trusting relationships and get people to see that they have more in common than they might think. Alexis Herman's test of leadership came just a few months after she became Secretary of Labor. In August of 1997, United Parcel workers belonging to the Teamsters Union began a bitter strike that threatened to shut down businesses across the country that were dependent on UPS delivery services. The new Labor Secretary brought both sides together but the talks broke down and her effort to get them going again were rebuffed. There were murmurs in the media and in government and labor circles that Alexis Herman might not be tough enough for the job. "Herman has no experience negotiating hard-core, labor-management disputes, and this is turning out to be an especially bitter one," *Newsweek* reported.

The Teamsters were tough, but Alexis's motto holds that "Failure is not an option." She waded into the power struggle between the workers and UPS management and once again brought both sides together for negotiations. It took a lot of intense work and long days and nights. To understand the issues better, the former social worker became an instant authority on the weight limits of UPS packages and other industry arcana. Both sides came to respect her effort to understand their positions. And after fifteen days, Alexis succeeded in ending the biggest strike in the United States in nearly two decades. In the process, she won over her critics and doubters, and established herself as a Life Brand leader of limitless potential.

"Labor sources yesterday lauded Herman for playing the classic role of mediator during the negotiations by keeping both sides talking, even when things got heated," noted the *Washington Post.* Even the Teamsters leaders who had opposed her nomination as Labor Secretary rated Alexis's performance during the UPS strike as "a 9, if not a 9.5" and told reporters that they were "extremely impressed by her presence."

"There's a grace that she has. It's the key to why she is so good at the interpersonal stuff," said one union official. The head of the AFL-CIO called her "a phenomenally quick study." And so there was Alexis Herman, daughter of a Mobile mortician and a reading teacher, sitting in the great theater of national government while everyone around applauded her contributions and recognized her leadership value. It doesn't get any better than that, does it?

## LEADERSHIP IS BUILT ON TRUSTING RELATIONSHIPS

I have encouraged you to identify and develop your talents, skills, and knowledge in order to build a Life Brand that adds something of value to everyone and everything you come into contact with in your work, your relationships, and your communities. Alexis Herman did that, and then she took her brand to a higher level. She became a Life Brand leader. Her greatest asset is not her fine mind or her ability to work long hours, or her understanding of political and governmental processes. It is her ability to earn the trust of others by demonstrating that she values their interests as much or more than her own.

Every powerful, leading Life Brand that I'm aware of—from Oprah to Quincy Jones, to Maya Angelou and Michael Jordan—was created through the efforts of not just the individual, but also many, many people who helped along the way.

It is your ability to build lasting and mutually supportive relationships—not your knowledge, or your athletic abilities, or your individual talents—that marks you as a Life Brand leader.

When you have established your trustworthiness and your interest in the welfare of others, you then have the leverage to influence the actions of people around you. What do I mean by *leverage?* When you talk about using leverage in a mechanical sense, you are talking about using a tool that gives you more power to accomplish a task. It's easier to remove a nail with the head of a hammer because the prongs give you more leverage, or power. You might try all day to remove a lug nut by hand from your car's tire, but you can do it with little effort with a lug wrench that gives you more leverage. In the same way, you can often get more leverage in your profession and your community—and sometimes in relationships too—when you can call upon the assistance of people whose success circle is greater than yours in certain areas.

I'd like to make an important point before we leave this consideration of Life Brands, relationships, and leadership. There is a huge difference between leveraging established relationships for mutual benefit and simply using others for your personal gain. One is the mark of a Life Brand leader, the other is a mark of a manipulator. I don't advocate that anyone set out to curry favor or win the friendship of another person solely for the purpose of using that person to further his or her goals. People who use others don't often enjoy long-term success or long-term friendships. Sooner or later, people revolt against manipulators by finding leaders who support their interests. Leadership is not about using other people, it's about building trust by showing concern for others, and living with honesty and integrity.

# The Power of Your Life Brand in the Community

CHAPTER TEN

MY FRIEND TOLBERT Chisum came from a family with a rich history, but little material wealth. His rugged cowboy ancestors created the famed Chisum-Goodnight Trail that allowed the cattle trade to flourish in the early days of the American West, but Tolbert had to carve out his own path as one of five children of a Sour Lake, Texas, oil field worker and his wife.

His father died when Tolbert was thirteen years old, so his mother was left to support their large family. They were difficult times. Yet, he became the first in his family to get a college degree, enjoyed a very successful career as an insurance sales executive, and later became one of the founders of North Shore Community Bank & Trust Company, a group of six banks with thirty locations in the Chicago area. Tolbert is now the managing director of their trust company, Wintrust Asset Management Company, in Winnetka, Illinois, and a man known for his service to others and to his community.

I've been involved with a great many nonprofit service and charitable organizations, and I've noticed that the people who seem to give the most of their talents and time are those who've known difficulty themselves. Tolbert is one of these people. Just a few years ago he was named one of the Top Ten Volunteers in the Chicago area. It didn't surprise me, because Athletes Against Drugs is one of the many organizations to benefit from Tolbert's community service. He is the chairman of our board of directors and a valued member of our organization.

One of the amazing things about Tolbert is that his days appear to have more hours than mine. There is no other explanation for all of the time he devotes to serving others. I came across his résumé recently, and found that he is actively involved in the Kenilworth Union Church, the Heartland Alliance (formerly Travelers and Immigrants Aid), and the Samaritan Institute. In addition, he serves as the unpaid village clerk for the suburb of Kenilworth, in which he lives. He does all of this even though his day job as a banking executive is not exactly part-time work.

Tolbert has created an exceptional life based on a philosophy of continuously working to add to the value of the lives of people around him. I believe you could fill a stadium with men and women who have benefited from his generosity, kindness, and concern for other people. Over the years I've known him, Tolbert has explained to me how he developed his Life Brand with its focus on community service, and I want to share his story with you. I believe that to build a truly great Life Brand—one that will leave a legacy—you have to use your gifts to benefit others. I feel that we should dedicate ourselves to causes greater than our own self-interests, but I also think that when you follow that philosophy, you often reap many unexpected rewards. Tolbert is one of my role models for this. His efforts to add value to the lives of others have given him a Life Brand of the highest quality.

Tolbert seems so confident and comfortable with himself today, I was surprised to learn that he was insecure and unhappy as a younger man. When he reached his early thirties, he realized that his life had veered off track. He had become so focused on attaining the material wealth he had not known as a child, he neglected his spiritual life and the Christian principles he'd grown up with. "As a boy, I didn't realize how poor we were because I had nothing to compare our situation to. Ignorance was bliss in some respects," he said. "But as I became an adult I began to realize what others had, and I became determined to make more and more money. Then, as I became successful financially, I realized I really wasn't happy. People were telling me that I was a great guy and a success, but I didn't feel good about myself."

Tolbert worked for one of the nation's largest insurance companies for twenty-seven years before he became a banker. He was an aggressive insurance salesman, eager to learn and succeed. His job was to sell group insurance, pensions, and employee benefit plans to businesses. He was taught to peddle as much coverage as his customers would buy and to collect the biggest premiums possible. Tolbert learned his lessons well. In his first few years, he became one of the top salesmen for his company. He earned more money than he had ever dreamed of making.

Still, he realized he wasn't happy with himself or with his work. "At first I thought that I was in the wrong business, so I explored a few other opportunities, but then I decided it wasn't the business that was the problem. It was an excellent company, but I didn't like playing by the rules that I'd been taught for selling their products. I'd become successful by their rules and not by mine as a good Christian," Tolbert recalled. "Rather than pushing for the highest premiums, I was much more comfortable selling policies and plans at the most reasonable and fair rate for everybody concerned. I preferred to put the customer's interests first. I decided that if I was going to stay in the insurance business, I was going to focus on providing maximum value to my customers. I wanted to quit pushing products that I didn't think were truly beneficial to my customers, and instead start doing things the way I would want somebody to take care of me and my business."

Tolbert wasn't sure how his decision would affect his career. He thought his earnings might slip, or he might be fired, but he was determined to change his approach because his conscience would not let him continue that way of life. In defiance of his coaching on salesmanship, Tolbert began counseling his customers to cut back on some of their coverage, because it was excessive. As a result, they began paying less in premiums to the insurance company.

Tolbert's own pay was tied to how much money he brought in, but even though many of his customers were paying less, his earnings began to soar. Why? "When I changed my approach my sales went through the roof," he recalled. "My clients gave me their absolute trust when they saw that I was willing to put their interests first. When people trust you, wonderful things happen. My clients began insisting that I meet their friends and handle their insurance business too."

Soon, Tolbert had more clients than ever before. His annual sales went from about $1 million to more than *$100 million,* and he became an even bigger star within his company. His success at work inspired Tolbert to apply his philosophy of helping others first in the community too. As a result, his influence and his good works expanded even more. "Too often, people don't realize that when you dedicate your life to giving value to others, it works for you too," he said. "You become healthier, happier, and more effective because people see that you are trustworthy. It simply makes for a better life."

Tolbert told me that he did not consciously set out to build a quality Life Brand in his work, his relationships (he has been married to Carrie, his high school sweetheart, for thirty-five years), and his community, but that is exactly what happened. "Your brand is built upon who you are and what you do," he said. "I always tried my dead level best to do the right thing, and so my brand came to represent as close to absolute trustworthiness as you can get. That is the secret of my success. People trust me because I work hard to earn their trust. In the community, I've built a brand as someone who wants to give back. I've found that the happiest people I meet are those who are givers, not takers."

## REACH OUT TO SHARE YOUR GIFTS AND REAP LONG-TERM REWARDS

The word *community* is derived from the Latin word *communis*, which means *common*. Your community, then, includes all of those people who have something in common with you whether it's the place you live, the sort of work you do, the interests you have, or the activities you enjoy. While the people who are closest to you are undoubtedly part of your community, so are many others who may simply be acquaintances or people you see only occasionally.

Today, our communities are far-flung and diverse. They might include those who share church affiliation or membership in special interest or hobby groups, networking and political organizations, and athletic leagues. Your extended community might also include Internet chat groups, charities and public service groups, social and investment clubs, government bodies, and neighborhood, community, state, or national organizations.

Having a strong Life Brand is extremely important in the wider circle of community, because many people may know you only by your reputation. They don't have the opportunity to observe your everyday actions or to talk to you personally, so their impression of you comes from others. If your brand is well developed, people outside your inner circle of friends and family won't have to speculate about you or form impressions from afar. They'll know what you stand for. And they will know what value you add to the community.

## BUILDING VALUE WHILE PROVIDING VALUE

When Stephen Lee, a senior vice president for a public relations firm in Cleveland, offered to serve on the board of the city ballet, he was asked quite bluntly whether he was truly interested in helping the Cleveland Ballet, or did he intend to simply use his position on its board to generate business for his employer. "If I contribute something to the organization, it certainly reflects well on myself and my firm. It can't hurt," was his reported answer.

That's right. It can't hurt your Life Brand for you to share your talents, gifts, and knowledge in the wider circles of the communities you belong to—unless, of course, your *only* motive is to help yourself or your career. I've known a few people who've volunteered to work in community groups for that selfish reason, and sooner or later, their self-serving motives become apparent and they either leave or depart upon request. That doesn't do anyone any good.

On the other hand, if you are willing to invest your time and effort seriously and give value to something bigger than yourself, it's been proven many times that you will reap benefits too; if not financial rewards, there are generally spiritual ones. There was controversy in Cleveland because of a company there called Business Volunteers Unlimited, which helped Stephen Lee hook up with the city ballet's volunteer board. For a fee of $1,500, this company plays matchmaker between businesses that want their employees to serve on community organizations and those nonprofit groups looking for talented volunteers. "The practice of advancing one's personal or business interests by joining a charitable board has been around for decades—as has the understanding that board membership can be contingent on being able to attract financial resources. But what's new here is the emergence of an actual broker that charges a fee for placing clients on nonprofit boards. Critics call it crass; boosters call it a service whose time has come," reported *The Wall Street Journal*.

There were legitimate fears in Cleveland that companies were using the service of Business Volunteers Unlimited solely for the purpose of having their employees network within the nonprofits to drum up business. "Networking is the worst reason to go on a nonprofit because then you care more about who's sitting next to you than the cause you're supposed to be helping," an expert in nonprofit groups told *The Wall Street Journal*.

The newspaper found instead that most of the nonprofit organizations that received placements from Business Volunteers were happy with the way things worked out. Many of the businesspeople "matched" to nonprofit groups by the service have wound up providing valuable assistance and serving in long-term leadership positions. The city's Health Museum, for example, was decrepit, outdated, and in bad financial shape until a Business Volunteer "match" from a nationwide consulting firm became chairman of its strategic-planning committee. His expertise and contacts helped bring about a major renovation effort. Similarly, the Near West Theatre, an inner-city youth program, and the Children's Museum of Cleveland were also revitalized by corporate volunteers recommended by the company.

"From overhauling board procedures, grooming or tossing out existing leadership, and launching multimillion-dollar expansions, board members championed by Business Volunteers are altering the city's philanthropic landscape," noted *The Wall Street Journal* reporter. "A big part of the appeal . . . turns out to be how deeply devoted many of the 'placed' trustees become to the organizations they join, regardless of their initial motives . . . Young executives, who are accustomed to flying around the world as hot-shot consultants on multimillion-dollar projects, come face-to-face with real problems in their own backyards and 'become human again . . . ' "

I'm not at all surprised. Once they begin doing community service work, even those people with mostly selfish motives discover the spiritual rewards of using their talents for a worthy cause. If you want to leave a legacy, if you want there to be more to remember you by than a cemetery plot and a headstone, then you have to think about creating a Life Brand that adds value beyond your immediate success circles.

As I mentioned in the previous chapter, corporations increasingly are encouraging their employees to devote time to community service, and some even pay them while they are doing it. The trend has not gone unnoticed by the universities and colleges that train and prepare young people for the workforce. In 1996, Olivet College in south-central Michigan became the first school in the nation to offer scholarships to students based on their records of community service in high school. Olivet offers a Community Responsibility Scholarship worth $6,000 a year as part of the small school's drive to encourage students to build Life Brands that offer value to the world around them. Other schools, universities, and colleges across the country are also increasing their emphasis on community service. Many thousands of high school and college students now spend their spring breaks working with Habitat for Humanity, helping with disaster relief, or serving the needs of their own communities.

I've been inspired by the community-minded people I've met over the years. When you do good things for others, it's like throwing a stone into a pond; the circles keep expanding and expanding. Often good deeds come back to touch your life too.

## A LIFE BRAND OF DIGNITY AND SERVICE TO OTHERS

LaMetta Wynn of Clinton, Iowa, worked the third shift at a hospital for more than twenty years while her husband, Thomas, worked days at the Rock Island Arsenal in order to put their ten children through high school and college. LaMetta rarely missed any of her youngsters' sporting or school events even though, in addition to her full-time job, she served for twelve years on the local school board—three years as its president. "I wanted to repay the community for the good educations my children were receiving and I couldn't think of any other way to do it other than serving on the school board, where I tried to make sure other children got the same opportunities," she said.

It's not surprising that Wynn's children grew up to become doctors, lawyers, nurses, police officers, and business professionals. What may be surprising is that after they grew into adulthood, their mother did not retire from serving her community. Instead, at the age of sixty-two, she ran for mayor. Again.

You see, the first time LaMetta ran for mayor was in 1993. She was still on the school board at that time, but she promised to give up her seat if she was elected. She lost. Many people in the community believe Clinton's teachers did not want LaMetta Wynn to quit the school board, where she was widely respected, so they voted for her mayoral opponent. They liked her so much, they voted against her.

When she ran again for mayor in 1995, her term on the school board had expired. That time, LaMetta beat out four other candidates, including the incumbent mayor, and captured 53 percent of the vote. Her victory was all the more impressive when you consider that LaMetta is a black woman, her opponents were all white males, and Clinton, Iowa, is less than 4 percent African-American, in a state that is 97 percent white!

LaMetta Wynn is a woman of great dignity with a long record of serving her community through quiet, highly principled leadership. When she asked for their support, the people of Clinton responded eagerly because of the value of her Life Brand. "She had this demeanor that said every problem could be solved," Clinton school superintendent Ben Trochlil told an interviewer. "She'd say, 'Let's not get carried away by the excitement of the problem until we get the facts first.' "

A reporter once asked Mayor Wynn if she was surprised she had become the first black woman to be elected mayor in the state of Iowa. Her answer shows, once again, why she is so well regarded by the people in her town. She said she had never given the racial issue much thought. "I'm just an ordinary person who tried to raise kids and do the best I could," she said. "I think if you are in a community and the community has been good to you, you should return something."

When I asked LaMetta to describe her brand, she came up with an answer that was typical of her humble spirits, and her good humor too. "I think of myself as all-purpose flour," she said. "I'm a little bland, but people seem to think I can do anything. I do have integrity, I think. I believe you always have to be true to yourself, and to your family, and try not to do things you will be sorry for. I also think that it's important to reach out if you think you have something to offer. You might just surprise yourself, and do something impossible, something you never dreamed of doing."

In late 1999, LaMetta was preparing to run for her second term as mayor of Clinton. Her Life Brand is so strong that she had no opposition this time around. "You'd be surprised at the number of people who say with a straight face that I ought to run for governor," she said. "But then I look at what Jesse Ventura did over in Minnesota and I think, Well, maybe I should."

There are great benefits to be derived from expanding your Life Brand to support causes greater than your own. I've certainly benefited enormously from my work with a wide range of charities and civic organizations. There are also a few important things to consider when offering your services. I've compiled them here for your consideration.

## GUIDELINES FOR EXPANDING YOUR LIFE BRAND INTO COMMUNITY SERVICE

1. *Focus on providing value to others, not on getting it for yourself.*
   It's true that public service and volunteer work can be a great way to network and market your skills, but self-service should never be your primary reason for public service. If others in the organization or community see that your motives are strictly self-serving, then you probably won't do yourself any good either. Instead, devote yourself to helping others with the idea that the ultimate benefit you hope to derive is the satisfaction of dedicating your talents and energy to a cause greater than yourself. Your greatest reward will be leaving a legacy that will have a positive impact on the world even after you are gone.

2. *Start in the trenches and stay there, even if you end up on the board.*
   Any time you join a service organization, you should keep in mind that the emphasis is on *service*. You will have the greatest impact by helping with the real work that is required. It's not called a service buffet. You don't get to stand back and pick whatever you want to do. You should be willing to pitch in with any and all of your resources. Of course, you don't want to get in over your head, so be honest about what you can handle. That's better than overpromising and underdelivering. If an organization asks you to do more than you have the time, talent, or resources

to do, be candid with them so that they can find someone else to do the job.

3. *Let your work speak for itself.*

I have cautioned you throughout the book that the process of building a Life Brand is not about self-promotion. It's about building value into your life. When you offer your services to your community, to organizations, or to any cause greater than yourself, let your actions speak for themselves. Do not promote yourself or your work within the group. If your efforts are worthy of praise and attention, they will come.

4. *Identify needs that match your special skills and interests.*

In my early days of community service, I often made the mistake of agreeing to get involved in organizations and projects for which I had little natural interest or expertise. Again, that really doesn't serve anyone. I now make certain that before I commit to an organization or a project its goals fit within my own Success Circles. Most of the organizations I am involved with work with young people or incorporate athletics in some way, so that they match up with my long-term goals.

5. *Commit to the cause.*

One of the most aggravating and frustrating aspects of public service work is dealing with people who make promises that they have no intention of keeping. It wastes the time and resources of the organization if "volunteers" and "donors" fail to walk the talk. It also does nothing to help their Life Brand image in the community. You might be surprised how quickly word spreads to the private sector if you fail to deliver on promises made to do public service work.

## WHERE TO LOOK FOR
## COMMUNITY SERVICE WORK

Your local City Hall or Chamber of Commerce should have a listing of service and charitable organizations in need of volunteers. You might also contact local houses of worship, the YMCA, YWCA, Boys and Girls Clubs, Boy Scouts and Girl Scouts, Big Brothers/Big Sisters of America, United Way, Junior Achievement, Salvation Army, Habitat for Humanity, American Red Cross, or service organizations such as the Lions, Rotary, or Kiwanis clubs. Here is a list of national public service organizations that can provide you with information for regional or local affiliates if you are seeking to get involved with a cause greater than yourself.

*Volunteers of America*
110 South Union Street
Alexandria, VA 22314-3351
1-800-899-0089
E-mail: voa@voa.org

Volunteers of America was founded in 1896 by Christian social reformers Ballington and Maud Booth as a broad spiritual movement to "reach and uplift" the American people. This is one of the nation's oldest, largest, and most comprehensive nonprofit human service organizations, which helps more than 1 million Americans every year, according to its Web site. Volunteers of America's community-based service organizations offer more than 160 programs. They help children, youths, the elderly, families in crisis, the homeless, the disabled, the mentally ill, and ex-offenders returning to society. In addition, Volunteers of America is the nation's largest nonprofit provider of affordable housing for low-income families and the elderly, and provides skilled long-term nursing care and other health services.

### Points of Light Foundation
1400 I Street N.W.
Suite 800
Washington, D.C. 20005
202-729-8000
E-mail: Volnet@pointsoflight.org

This is a nonpartisan, nonprofit organization devoted to promoting volunteerism. The foundation is based in Washington, D.C., and works in communities throughout the United States through a network of over 500 Volunteer Centers. The foundation believes that at the core of most social problems lie disconnection and alienation. That is why the foundation launched an initiative called Connect America, which is designed to unite people through volunteer service.

### America's Promise—The Alliance for Youth
909 North Washington Street
Suite 400
Alexandria, VA 22314-1556
703-535-3900
E-mail: local@americaspromise.org

This organization is led by retired General Colin Powell. It is dedicated to mobilizing individuals, groups, and organizations from every part of American life, to build and strengthen the character and competence of our youth. Its goal is to point children in the right direction, to help them grow up strong and ready to take their places as successful adults.

> *Global Service Corps*
> 300 Broadway Suite 28
> San Francisco, CA 94133
> 415-788-3666 Extension 128
> E-mail: gsc@igc.org

GSC provides opportunities for people of all ages who want to share their time and experience to help make the world a better place, according to its Web site. GSC participants live and work in developing countries, such as Costa Rica, Thailand, or Kenya, and take part in a wide range of projects designed to improve the well-being of the Earth and its inhabitants. At the same time, participants gain a whole new perspective on the world.

> *Impact Online*
> 325 B Forest Avenue
> Palo Alto, CA 94301
> 650-327-1389
> Web Site: www.impactonline.org

Founded in 1994, Impact Online is a nonprofit organization dedicated to increasing volunteerism through the Internet. IOL offers VolunteerMatch, a matching service for volunteers and nonprofits; Virtual Volunteering, a research project on volunteer activities which can be completed over the Internet; and information and resources on volunteerism. According to the information provided on its Web site, which has won numerous awards, Impact Online's VolunteerMatch places thousands of volunteers with nonprofits. Its Web site receives nearly 25,000 visitors each month.

### World SHARE Incorporated
Regional offices in 15 states
888-742-7372
Web Site: www.worldshare.org

World SHARE (Self-Help and Resource Exchange) is a nonprofit social business serving a multinational network of organizations. In the United States, World SHARE works through regional programs called "SHARE affiliates" to promote community participation. The SHARE affiliates reward people who volunteer in their communities with up to 50 percent savings on food. Active in fifteen states, SHARE affiliates work with volunteers at churches, schools, senior centers, and other social organizations to distribute this low-cost food. Each month, more than 250,000, U.S. families help their communities and take advantage of significant savings on food through SHARE.

### Corporation for National Service
1201 New York Avenue, N.W.
Washington, D.C. 20525
202-606-5000
E-mail: webmaster@cns.gov
Web Site: www.cns.gov

The CNS traces its heritage of national service back to a speech given in 1910 by American philosopher William James, who envisioned a nonmilitary national service. Its predecessors include the Civilian Conservation Corps, formed under

President Franklin D. Roosevelt; the Peace Corps, created under President John F. Kennedy; and VISTA (Volunteers in Service to America), created by President Lyndon B. Johnson. The Corporation for National Service and AmeriCorps, which now includes VISTA, were created under the National and Community Service Trust Act of 1993 signed by President Bill Clinton.

The CNS carries on our nation's tradition of citizen volunteers by working with community organizations to provide opportunities for Americans of all ages to engage in community service. It includes three volunteer groups:

o AmeriCorps, which engages more than 40,000 Americans in intensive, results-driven service and then gives education awards to help finance college or pay back student loans to those who serve.
o Learn & Serve America, which has involved more than 1 million children as participants in service-learning activities in their schools and communities.
o National Senior Service Corps, which has assisted nearly half a million Americans age fifty-five or over in finding ways to share their time and talents to solve local problems.

The CNS Web site provides links to ServeNet, a useful, searchable database of volunteer opportunities, and IdeaList, a resource for volunteers.

# Seven Rules for Building a Quality Life Brand

CHAPTER ELEVEN

**The First Rule:** *Your Brand Can't Be All Things to All People*

Recently, I was asked to speak to a national environmental organization but I had to politely decline the invitation, just as I do many others from groups with special interests that are beyond my areas of expertise. I am concerned about the environment, of course, and I respect people who give their time and effort to protecting our natural resources. But I am not an authority on environmental issues. I do not speak to groups or topics that fall outside my areas of concentration in training and development, marketing, multicultural markets, or youth and community development. I've found in the past that it doesn't serve my audience, or my own goals, to speak outside those realms.

I would much rather spend that time becoming more knowledgeable and better skilled in the things that I am passionate about so that I can offer even more value in those arenas. I might make more in speaking fees if I accepted every invitation that came my way. I might even come upon some opportunities or meet some interesting people. But would *my* goals be served? Would my Life Brand benefit over the long term?

It is possible to become too aggressive and to extend your Life Brand so far that it loses its identity altogether. In general, the more focused your Life Brand is, the more powerful it will be over your lifetime. Most major celebrities like Tiger Woods and Mia Hamm sign long-term endorsement contracts with just a few major brands in order to keep their celebrity brands strong, though they might make even more money in the short term by making commercials and print ads for dozens of products. That's because they understand this rule. They know that it is smarter to take a little water from the well so that it can replenish itself, rather than trying to take out all the water at once and risk running it dry.

I was in New York City recently and saw an advertisement for a Harley-Davidson restaurant. A few days later, I saw another advertisement for Harley-Davidson wine coolers. If I owned stock in that company, I think I'd be concerned that it was pushing its powerful brand for a legendary motorcycle beyond its limits. Just as American Express diluted its brand by issuing dozens of different credit cards, I've seen other consumer products companies, and even many celebrities, extend their brands so far that it becomes difficult to identify them at all. And if people don't know what you stand for, why would they buy into your brand?

In the world of brands, from consumer products to celebrities and personal brands, there is no single brand that appeals to each and every individual or target market. Coca-Cola has one of the most powerful brands in the world, but there are many people who prefer Seven-Up or Dr Pepper or simply a glass of water. Michael Jordan has a powerful celebrity brand, but not everyone aspires to be an athlete or competitor "like Mike." Some prefer to be scholars or inventors or healers. The point is that no single brand can appeal to all people all of the time. So why try? Your goal should be to become the best at whatever it is you love to do, and then to build your Life Brand around it.

When you stretch your brand too far, you risk losing your ability to offer value to those around you. When I was younger, I thought I knew everything. If someone brought up a topic or a controversial issue of the day, I generally had an opinion to offer. Now, I am struck almost every day by how much there is that I still have to learn. The bit of knowledge that probably serves me best is the awareness that I cannot know everything and I cannot be all things to all people. I'm reminded of this whenever I get around a group of adolescent boys. They enthusiastically practice the rituals of manhood without the self-control of mature males. Like men, they trade stories and often try to one-up each other, but unlike most—but certainly not all—adults, the boys, in their eagerness to outshine each other, will wax on and on about people, places, and things of which they have no real knowledge. Sooner or later, they make themselves look foolish, or someone else does it for them.

Most men and women learn early on in their teenage years that you can't get away with trying to be master of all knowledge and that you can't be all things to all people. It is a lesson that is often learned the hard way. Many years ago, a Chicago television station manager thought that I had the makings of a TV news anchor. At that point in my life, I was still trying to decide what I wanted to do with myself, so I thought I'd give it a try. A few trial runs and a few played-back videos quickly helped me decide that I was not made for television. I just didn't have the necessary background in broadcasting and news reporting, nor was my heart in it. I might have considered becoming a sports broadcaster, but at that point in my life, I wasn't comfortable in front of the camera. I had no passion for it.

I believe that above all else, you should follow your passions by identifying the things you love to do and then building your work life around them. That is how you create a Quality Life Brand that inspires others and attracts opportunities over the course of a lifetime. It is all but impossible to build a Quality Life Brand while trying to be all things to all people because sooner or later, you end up doing things that don't mean anything to you. I might have been able to pull off a broadcasting job for a while, but I realized that sooner or later I would have tired of it. It just wasn't the direction I wanted to go. It wasn't the brand I wanted to build.

Chevrolet may have extended its brand by making a wide range of vehicles including economy cars, family cars, sports cars, SUVs, and trucks, but you don't see the car company venturing into refrigerators or stereos, do you? McDonald's has tried all sorts of menu items over the years, but time and again the fast-food franchise has decided to stick with the burgers and fries that have made it the most successful restaurant chain in history. They understand that there are people who may want a pizza, or ribs, or a steak dinner now and then, but McDonald's has decided that its great brand will not try to provide all things to all people. You shouldn't either.

Your parents may have mapped out your life based on their experiences and their concern for your financial welfare. Your friends may push you to do what they do in order to keep you close. Others who love you may wish for you to do what fits their vision of you. I advise you to follow your passions and look for opportunities linked to them. That is the way to build a Quality Life Brand and an enjoyable lifetime journey.

## The Second Rule:
### *Keep Stretching for Everything Within Your Grasp*

This second rule for building your Life Brand is a corollary to the first one. While you should never try to be all things to all people, you should certainly never stop stretching and reaching for everything within your grasp. The greatest Life Brands I am aware of are those that are far-reaching. These people never stop stretching their brand assets—their talents, knowledge, and skills—in order to keep growing and reaching new heights of achievement and fulfillment.

One of the best examples of this is Quincy Jones. His life serves as a model and an example for this second rule. Quincy's Life Brand is built around his primary interest in music. His focus, then, is relatively narrow, but his reach is extraordinary. One biography describes him as a "composer, record producer, artist, film producer, arranger, conductor, instrumentalist, TV producer, record company executive, magazine founder, and multi-media entrepreneur," but I don't think even that description captures the full range of his accomplishments.

Quincy grew up poor on Chicago's South Side and later moved to Seattle. He began playing the trumpet and singing in a gospel quartet at the age of twelve, and while he was a teenager he studied at the prestigious Berklee College of Music in Boston. He left school at the age of eighteen to tour with the famed band of Lionel Hampton as a trumpeter, arranger, and pianist. Just a few years later, he was a widely acclaimed arranger working with many of the biggest entertainers of the era, including Sarah Vaughan, Ray Charles, Count Basie, Duke Ellington, and Dinah Washington.

At this point in his life, Quincy did something that may have seemed risky at the time, but when you read the biographies of people with the most powerful Life Brands, you find it is actually quite common. Though he had achieved remarkable success at a very early age, Quincy decided to extend his reach by stepping outside the world of American jazz and exploring new musical ground. Unlike many other young people who have been anointed "geniuses" and let it go to their heads, Quincy felt he still had a great deal to learn, and so he moved to Paris to study with a legendary tutor named Nadia Boulanger, who had also mentored the famous American composers Leonard Bernstein and Aaron Copland.

I mentioned that Quincy's decision to add value to his already strong Life Brand was common for people with powerful brands. I'll give you another quick example from an entirely different realm. In 1990, after the Bulls were beaten in the NBA Conference Finals by the highly physical Detroit Pistons, Michael Jordan—who was already considered to be the best player in the league—hired his own personal trainer and began a carefully designed fitness regime to add ten pounds of muscle to his upper body. Some of his closest friends told Michael he was making a mistake by trying to change a body that had already taken him to stardom, but Jordan countered that he was getting "beaten to death" by stronger players on opposing teams.

Like Quincy, Michael could have settled for the gifts that he already had. No one was pushing him to get better than he already was. Except Michael himself. He went through a very difficult training program, privately, at his own expense, be-

cause he wanted to extend his reach. When Michael's teammates saw how his added strength improved his play, they
were inspired to begin their own weight training programs.
Their increased strength and confidence are credited with
helping the Bulls defeat Detroit on their way to winning the
first of six NBA championships.

Michael is now retired from basketball and, apparently,
his current focus is on becoming a great golfer. He was quoted
as saying that he is learning the fundamentals of the game
from professional Ray Floyd. I doubt that either Michael Jordan or Quincy Jones will ever quit reaching for new heights of
accomplishment. All powerful Life Brands are like that. They
are constantly searching for new ways to stretch themselves
and their talents and knowledge. What can you do to extend
your grasp? How can you increase the value of your Life
Brand? What can you do to bring more value to your work, to
your relationships, and to your community? These are questions that you should never stop asking yourself, because they
ignite your passions and they keep you alive mentally, emotionally, and spiritually.

## The Third Rule:
### *Think Long Term When Building a Life Brand*

I saw a disturbing statistic recently. It said residents in one of
the poorest neighborhoods in Chicago had invested more
than $70 million in the state lottery. That is a classic case of
people seeking short-term gains rather than building for
long-term success. You've heard it all before. We are a quick-
fix society. Instead of building wealth by investing and saving,
we buy lottery tickets. Rather than watching what we eat and

exercising regularly, we gobble vitamin supplements and weight-loss pills. Very few people win the lottery, but millions of Americans have built long-term wealth by investing wisely. The only proven method for losing weight and keeping it off over the long term is to eat carefully and exercise regularly.

The same principles apply to building, expanding, and managing your Life Brand. It is okay to set *short-term goals* that help you build your Life Brand step by step. I set many goals as I re-created my Life Brand, and as I met each one along the way, I created new goals. But I resisted the temptation to go for *short-term gains* that might have detracted from my Life Brand over the long term. You've seen some graphic examples of this in recent years with public figures and celebrities who have been publicly humiliated or suffered career setbacks after embarrassing photographs, videos, or other materials from their pasts have surfaced and damaged their brands. Often, those embarrassing materials were the result of something done for a short-term gain without regard for the long-term implications. In the same way, abusing drugs and alcohol may give a short-term boost or high, but those actions can also lead to addiction, criminal charges, and other long-term repercussions that can destroy a career and relationships.

On the other hand, many of the greatest Life Brands in history were created by those individuals who always kept their long-term goals in mind, even when they may have been sorely tempted to go for short-term gratification. Remember my earlier example of Nelson Mandela's refusing to accept the terms of freedom offered by his captors? He never lost sight of his long-term goal, though he surely must have yearned to be free. In the same way, I'm sure there must have been many days and nights when the Reverend Martin Luther King was tempted to leave the civil rights battlefields in Montgomery and Little Rock and return to the security and peace of his own church and family. He remained focused on his long-term goal of racial equality.

One of the great benefits of creating a Life Brand is that it helps you to always keep your lifelong goals in mind so that you stay on course to your dreams. Whenever you are tempted to go for a short-term gain, I advise you to think about the impact it might have on your Life Brand over the long term. I do it almost every day. It doesn't have to be a matter of life and death. It can be something as simple as telling off a coworker who has done something to offend you. Before you go for the short-term satisfaction of telling the coworker exactly what you think of him or her, give some thought to what the long-term implications might be on your Life Brand. Will venting your anger and frustration help your brand image around the office? Or would it be better to resolve your differences in a less confrontational manner? What action will best serve *your* Life Brand over the long term?

Do not underestimate the value of long-term thinking in the brand-building process. It can have a substantial impact even with seemingly small things no matter where you are in the cycle of life. A friend of mine told me his rather typical story of high school alienation that resulted from his refusal to smoke cigarettes with classmates who were part of the "in" crowd. He wasn't a goody-two-shoes by any means, but smoking just never appealed to him, so whenever he was offered a cigarette, he declined. It was many years later when he realized that whenever he was offered a cigarette, he unconsciously recalled an image of his grandmother, a heavy smoker, coughing and choking from the lung disease that eventually resulted in her death. Because he had unconsciously learned to associate smoking (a short-term "high") with death (the long-term result), he had no interest in it. His refusal to smoke may have caused him some short-term social problems, but over the long term it was good for his physical health and it won him the lasting respect of other classmates who admired his ability to resist peer pressure.

We all fall to temptations. We all find ways to justify doing things for short-term gains even when we know they may not serve our long-term interests. Sometimes, you will fall short. From time to time, we all do it, in small ways, and sometimes in big ways. We order the French fries instead of the tossed salad. We take the easy class instead of the more challenging one. We stay in bed instead of getting up to work out. We all have our weak moments and, to tell you the truth, I can't imagine life without an occasional bowl of ice cream or a lazy morning reading the newspapers and sipping juice. I'm not asking you to be perfect. That's too stressful, and probably boring too. But if you always keep your long-term goals in mind, I believe you'll stay on track and you will maintain the integrity of your Life Brand.

If you start each day by asking yourself, *What can I do today to build greater value into my Life Brand?* and keep that long-term thought in mind, I believe you will avoid the short-term traps that await us all. Long-term thinking allows you to stay focused on what matters most—not what might feel good right now, not what might produce a quick boost or a fast dollar. Wouldn't your life be better if you knew that every day you were moving closer to the goals and dreams that matter the most to you, those that will give you the greatest amount of personal satisfaction and spiritual reward over the long term? Then train yourself to think for the *long-term* when building, expanding, and managing your Life Brand.

## The Fourth Rule: *Market Your Brand, but Let It Sell Itself*

A friend told me the story of two people he met during his first year in high school. One of them, Randy, made a big splash in the first few days of their freshman year. Randy came from a small, rural grade school where he was a top athlete and a leader in his class. He was a strong, smart, good-looking kid. He could have been a standout in the class and a leader. But Randy didn't understand the principles behind this fourth rule. He oversold himself. Before the football season started, he bragged that he was going to be the starting quarterback. But when it came time to sign up for the team, he claimed that he failed the physical because of a childhood illness. He did try out for the basketball team after boasting that he'd been the top scorer on his grade school team. He didn't make the cut.

It wasn't long before his classmates wrote Randy off as a big talker who couldn't back up his claims. He found himself without many close friends, and he never did live up to his early promise as a class standout.

Then there was Jake. He came to my friend's high school from the same small, rural grade school as Randy. He was a big guy, quiet and friendly. He would sit back and watch Randy hold court in the first months of school, but he didn't join in the boasting. He did go out for the football team and he became known as a tough and determined player. He also went out for the basketball team, and although at first it was obvious that he had not played much, he worked hard on his game, staying late every night and coming in early each morning to work with the coaches. He became a starter in the second half of the season. Slowly, his classmates came to appreciate Jake's contributions. He became a leader both on and off the playing fields.

Randy and Jake came from similar backgrounds, but one focused on selling himself, while the other quietly worked to build value into his Life Brand while letting his actions speak for him. I asked my friend what became of his two classmates after high school. You won't be surprised at the results. Randy continued on a self-destructive path and, sadly, never fulfilled his promise. Jake married, raised a family, and became a successful businessman and community leader.

Life is not a sprint; it is a marathon. Randy didn't understand that. It's a difficult concept to grasp when you are young and eager to establish yourself. As I've noted, I was also guilty of overselling myself at that age. Fortunately, as an adult, I came to understand that the best way to market your brand is to focus on bringing value to your work, your relationships, and your community. When you do that, the marketing generally takes care of itself.

The best way to market your Life Brand is to be such a stand out that other people generate "the buzz" for you. Networking experts say that personal referrals or word-of-mouth recommendations generate 80 percent more results than sales calls to potential clients or customers.

There are plenty of ways to sell yourself in this media-mad world. You can take out newspaper ads, create a Web site, do a promotional video, or send out mass mailings advertising your products or services. Unless you offer real value, none of these methods is worth the cost.

What if you have worked to refine your talents and skills to a high level but no one recognizes them? What do you do then? Too many people look at those who have been successful and try to model their behavior after they've become successes, instead of modeling the actions that *made* them successes. If you look to the roots of their success, you'll likely find that they marketed themselves from the bottom up. For example, most successful journalists started on small newspapers or in low-profile jobs on larger publications. The most respected lawyers, accountants, doctors, artists, and businesspeople generally worked in the lower tiers of their professions to build their expertise and their reputations. All stars begin as specks of dust in the universe. It's their ability to attract and interact with other particles that eventually gives them power.

The marketing of your Life Brand begins with the person sitting next to you at work, in church, on the train, or in a hair salon. Your brand is built one person at a time. And it begins with you and the value that your Life Brand represents. Just as there are many ways to sell yourself, there are hundreds of ways to market yourself. If you feel that you need to expedite the process of building a Life Brand by marketing it, look to those places where you can add value. Look to your community. Your relationships. Your house of worship. Your professional organizations. When you give of your talents without expecting anything in return, the rewards come from the most unexpected places.

## The Fifth Rule: *Fortify Your Brand by Teaming Up*

When one of the most successful restaurateurs in the nation, Rich Melman of Chicago, was asked in an interview what his greatest strength is, he replied: "Surrounding myself with people who complement me. I'm painfully aware of what I don't do well."

As the owner of Lettuce Entertain You Enterprises, a

Chicago business empire that includes more than fifty restaurants, Rich Melman obviously has many talents both as a restaurateur and as a businessman. Yet, he understands that one of the most vital aspects of building a brand is teaming up with other Life Brands who make him even stronger. Having a strong team around him enables Melman to focus on his strengths, knowing that others will take care of those areas in which he may be weak.

Like him, I believe in building on my strengths and creating a support team to overcome any weaknesses. "One of the best ways I've found to keep enhancing your qualifications and fortifying your brand—is to build a network of talented people to think and grow with," branding consultant Lisa Gansky of Marketect told *Fast Company*. "Listen hard to the people you trust when they're responding to what you're doing."

I believe life is a team sport, and because of that, I think your time is best spent focusing on your strengths. That doesn't mean that you'll become a one-dimensional person. Quincy Jones focused on his musical composition skills early in his life and he is a modern Renaissance man. In fact, psychologists have found that developing a mastery in one area of life gives you the framework and confidence to master, or at least achieve competence in, other areas. Focusing on your weaknesses, however, will likely only bring frustration.

One of the greatest joys in life is doing something well, getting into the flow of an activity that you enjoy and have a mastery of, no matter what it is. Think about the happiest and most confident people you know. I'll bet most of them are people with an easily identifiable talent that they've built a life around. I'm sure they have weaknesses too, we all do, but they've made a conscious decision to focus on what they do best.

I read a biography recently of a boy who grew up being teased by his father and brother because he didn't have their mechanical skills. The father, who had been an airplane mechanic in the military, even told this son to "go in the house with the women" when he was working on a car because the boy just didn't have a knack for it. I think we all agree that the mechanically inept youngster, Michael Jordan, made a good decision when he decided to focus on his strengths as an athlete instead.

It can be tough to admit you don't have certain skills, but being honest in your self-appraisal can mark the difference between great success and mediocrity. I know of a very smart lawyer who nearly lost his job a few years ago because he was just not comfortable presenting a case to a jury. He loved doing trial work and he was brilliant at getting to the heart of a case and researching complex legal issues. But trial lawyers also must be skillful communicators, and this fellow wasn't. Even worse was the fact that for many years, he refused to acknowledge that he just didn't enjoy standing in front of a jury and making his case to them.

He was insecure about his lack of speaking skills and he didn't want his law partners to see his weakness. But they did. And it made for several years of tension within the law firm. Finally, a wise senior partner started talking to the troubled lawyer. He told him that his future as a trial lawyer with the firm was in jeopardy. "You are a brilliant legal tactician and we hate to lose a man of your talent, but you are simply not effective in the courtroom," the senior partner told him. Finally, he was forced to admit that he had tried to cover up his weaknesses and it had made him miserable. When the lawyer showed that he was willing to acknowledge his weaknesses, the senior partner saw that there was hope for him. He proposed that the lawyer join forces with another attorney in the firm who was known for his great courtroom presence but needed help in formulating legal strategies. Once they joined forces, with each man's strengths complementing the other's weaknesses, they became a highly successful team.

Build your brand on your strengths and you will find ways to overcome your weaknesses. Always remember that you don't have to be master of all things; you only have to look to others whose skills complement yours.

## The Sixth Rule:
### *The Strongest Life Brands Are Those That Lift Others Up*

A few years ago, I returned to my hometown of Whitesboro, New Jersey, and I was struck by how badly it had deteriorated and grown stagnant. It's a small town—a village, really—that was founded by George H. White, who was a pioneering African-American and a U.S. congressman. I was concerned because I still have relatives back there, both young and old. So I helped create a group called Concerned Citizens of Whitesboro with the goal of revitalizing the community and restoring pride. We've been able to get streets and sidewalks repaired. We started a local festival to get people more involved in the town. We've begun to restore a sense of community. One of the best things to come out of the organization is that it helped many of the young people in Whitesboro see that they could make a difference. In fact, one young lady has decided to run for public office so that she can work within the system to improve the lives of people in the community.

Throughout this book, I have stressed that the secret to building a Quality Life Brand is to focus on bringing value to the world around you. To your work. To your loved ones. To all of the communities in which you are involved. You won't be remembered for what you took out of this world; you will be remembered for what you left behind. The most honored Life Brands in history are those of individuals who rose above by reaching out. One of those people, the Reverend Martin Luther King, Jr., said, "The power of service is that anyone can serve." There is no greater power available to you and me, either materially or spiritually. Reverend King is one example of that. He rose from the pastor of the Dexter Avenue Baptist Church in Montgomery, Alabama, to leader of the civil rights movement, which changed this nation for the better, and inspired the world. Although he was killed by an assassin in 1968, his Life Brand is still a powerful influence on the public consciousness and the causes of social justice and civil rights around the world.

A small-town, sickly child from Cedarville, Illinois, offers another example of the power of service. Jane Addams came to Chicago in 1889, at a time when most educated people believed that the best way to help the poor was to preach temperance and faith to them. Jane believed that "the world grows better because people wish that it should and take the right steps to make it better." Although her father was wealthy and her own health was poor, she didn't choose to live a pampered life. Instead, she moved into one of the city's worst disease-ridden slums to work among the city's immigrant poor. There, she cofounded Hull House, and over the course of her lifetime she created the field of social work. She pioneered in the building of public playgrounds and swimming pools. She trained poor men and women so they could find work, and then she created labor unions to protect them. She worked for laws to protect abused women, children, and infants.

Jane Addams became the first woman to win a Nobel Prize, but more important is the legacy she left behind. More than 100 years after Jane Addams came to Chicago and more than 65 years after her death, her Life Brand is still incredibly powerful. The Jane Addams Hull House Association serves more than 225,000 people in the Chicago area each year, continuing her goal to elevate the lives of the city's underprivileged men, women, and children.

We all have things we want to accomplish in our lifetimes, but you should always keep in mind the legacy that you will leave. What will your lasting impact be upon your chosen line of work and the people you work with, the people you love, and those in all of the communities to which you belong? If you always keep that question in mind when making decisions as to the direction of your life, you will build a Life Brand that may inspire others long after you are gone.

## The Seventh Rule: *Build Joy into Your Life Brand!*

I've given you a lot to think about, and a lot to do, in this book. My goal is to help you become the conscious manager of your own life. In creating a Life Brand, you establish a process for taking control of not only your image but of your entire journey through the challenging days and nights of your time here on this planet.

I lost my father a few years ago, and recently a friend of mine lost his father too. We both have reflected on their lives, and we both came away with the thought that one of the wisest things we can do to honor the memory of our fathers is to make the most of the time we've been given. That means doing all we can to identify, develop, and use up our gifts for the highest possible purpose—to dedicate our lives to things greater than ourselves. It also means taking joy in every second, every minute, and every hour allotted to us.

Do you do that? Do you take time to appreciate the gifts that each day gives to you? I'm not referring to material things. What meaning do they really have for you? I'm speaking about far greater gifts. The laughter of a child. The beauty of a fall day. The pleasure of a good book. The first taste of an ice cream cone. Simple pleasures offer great rewards when you view them in wide perspective. Take joy where you find it. Take it in the greatest doses available. View the world with wide eyes and a curious mind. Never stop laughing, wondering, imagining, growing, or giving of yourself.

We have only so much time to share our gifts and to leave something of value for others to find and build upon. I sincerely hope that the material in this book has enhanced your ability to do that. I wish you joy and happiness as you build your powerful Life Brand.

# PUBLICATIONS AND SERVICES:
# S. GRAHAM & ASSOCIATES

## PUBLICATIONS

- Graham, Stedman. *You Can Make It Happen: A Nine-Step Plan for Success.* New York: Simon & Schuster, 1997. Hardbound: $23.00
- Graham, Stedman. *You Can Make It Happen: A Nine-Step Plan for Success.* Audio Book. New York: Simon & Schuster, 1997. Audio: $18.00
- Graham, Stedman. *You Can Make It Happen: A Nine-Step Plan for Success.* New York: Simon & Schuster, 1998. Softbound: $12.00
- Graham, Stedman. *You Can Make It Happen Every Day.* New York: Simon & Schuster, 1998. Softbound: $10.00
- Graham, Stedman. *Teens Can Make It Happen: Nine Steps to Success.* New York: Simon & Schuster/Fireside, 2000. Softbound: $14.00
- Graham, Stedman, Joe Jeff Goldblatt, and Lisa Delpy Neirotti. *The Ultimate Guide to Sports Marketing.* McGraw-Hill, 2001. Hardbound: $24.95
- Graham, Stedman. *Build Your Own Life Brand!* New York: Simon & Schuster/Free Press, May 2001. Hardbound: $25.00

## SERVICES

Stedman Graham is available for speaking engagements and presentations at corporate meetings, regional and national gatherings. His company, S. Graham & Associates, provides customized corporate training and leadership development programs. For additional information, contact S. Graham & Associates at (312) 755-0234.